W9-DGW-551

GATHER YOUR STRENGTH, SISTERS:
THE EMERGING ROLE OF
CHINESE WOMEN COMMUNITY WORKERS

IMMIGRANT COMMUNITIES & ETHNIC MINORITIES IN THE UNITED STATES & CANADA: No. 24

ISSN 0749–5951

Series Editor: Robert J. Theodoratus

Department of Anthropology, Colorado State University

1. James G. Chadney. *The Sikhs of Vancouver.* 1984
2. Paul Driben. *We Are Metis: The Ethnography of a Halfbreed Community in Northern Alberta.* 1985
3. a. Michael Colfer. *Morality, Kindred, and Ethnic Boundary: A Study of the Oregon Old Believers.* 1985
4. Nanciellen Davis. *Ethnicity and Ethnic Group Persistance in an Acadian Village in Maritime Canada.* 1985
5. Juli Ellen Skansie. *Death Is for All: Death and Death-Related Beliefs of Rural Spanish-Americans.* 1985
6. Robert Mark Kamen. *Growing Up Hasidic: Education and Socialization in the Bobover Hasidic Community.* 1985
7. Liuccija Baskauskas. *An Urban Enclave: Lithuanian Refugees in Los Angeles.* 1985
8. Manuel Alers-Montalvo. *The Puerto Rican Migrants of New York City.* 1985
9. Wayne Wheeler. *An Analysis of Social Change in a Swedish-Immigrant Community: The Case of Lindsborg, Kansas.* 1986
10. Edwin B. Almirol. *Ethnic Identity and Social Negotiation: A Study of a Filipino Community in California.* 1985
11. Stanford Neil Gerber. *Russkoya Celo: The Ethnography of a Russian-American Community.* 1985
12. Peter Paul Jonitis. *The Acculturation of the Lithuanians of Chester, Pennsylvania.* 1986
14. Dorothy Ann Gilbert. *Recent Portuguese Immigrants to Fall River, Massachusetts: An Analysis of Relative Economic Success.* 1989
15. Jeffrey Lynn Eiphney. *Mennonite Architecture: Diachronic Evidence for Rapid Diffusion in Rural Communities.* 1989
16. Elizabeth Kathleen Briody. *Houshold Labor Patterns among Mexican Americans in South Texas: Buscando Trabajo Seguro.* 1989
17. Karen L. S. Muir. *The Strongest Part of the Family: A Study of Lao Refugee Women in Columbus, Ohio.* 1988
19. Mary G. Harris. *Cholas: Latino Girls and Gangs.* 1988.
22. Bruce LaBrack. *The Sikhs of Northern California, 1904–1975: A Socio-Historical Study.* 1988
24. Stacey G. H. Yap. *Gather Your Strength, Sisters: The Emerging Role of Chinese Women Community Workers.* 1989
25. Phyllis Cancilla Martinelli. *Ethnicity In The Sunbelt: Italian-American Migrants in Scottsdale, Arizona.* 1989
28. Marilyn Preheim Rose. *On The Move: A Study of Migration and Ethnic Persistence among Mennonites from East Freeman, South Dakota.* 1989
30. Bernard Wong. *Patronage, Brokerage, Entrepreneurship and the Chinese Community of New York.* 1988

GATHER YOUR STRENGTH, SISTERS
THE EMERGING ROLE OF
CHINESE WOMEN COMMUNITY WORKERS

Stacey G. H. Yap

AMS Press
New York

Library of Congress Cataloging-in-Publication Data

Yap, Stacey G. H.
  Gather your strength, sisters.

  (Immigrant communities & ethnic minorities in the United
States & Canada 24)
  Bibliography: p.
  Includes index.
  1. Women in community development—United States—
Case studies. 2. Chinese American women—Case
studies. 3. Chinese Americans—Social conditions—Case
studies. I. Title. II. Series.
HQ1240.5.U6Y36 1989   307.1'4'089951   87-45789
ISBN 0-404-19434-6

All AMS books are printed on acid-free paper that meets
the guidelines for performance and durability of the Committee on Production Guidelines for Book Longevity of the
Council on Library Resources.

AMS PRESS
56 East 13th Street
New York, N.Y. 10003, U.S.A.

Manufactured in the United States of America

CONTENTS

Preface ix

Introduction 1

Chapter

I. Northville Chinatown 8

II. The Emergence of Community Work 25

III. Getting Involved: The Lives and Work of Community Workers 43

IV. Networking 86

V. Hard Work 104

VI. Women of Valor 121

VII. Conclusions: Summary and Implications 129

Appendixes

A. Sample Backgrounds and Characteristics 139

B. Types of Organizations 143

C. On the Methods Used in this Study 146

Notes 162

Selected Bibliography 167

Index 173

LIST OF TABLES

Table

1. Linkages of Subtypes of Community Workers 92

2. The Life Patterns of Community Workers 130

LIST OF ILLUSTRATIONS

Figure

1. Map of Northville Chinatown 9

2. Historical Development of Community Work in Northville Chinatown ... 26

3. Social Linkages of the Women Community Workers 90

4. Intensity of Participation by Types of Community Workers 161

For My Mother,

Madam Tan Kok Ho

謹以本書獻給吾母
陳菊好女士

PREFACE

"Northville" Chinatown and the community workers are still very active in 1986. The Northville's newspaper, North Star reported in 1985 that the Chinese community has seen many different groups, and yet "...never have we been so united" in rallying around issues and encouraging direct participation from the Chinese people. Although some community workers have left Northville since the study has been completed, community work still remains visible and important. For example, the community work of "Emily" flourishes. In May 1986, she led 350 laid-off Chinese garment workers to the State House to demand job training and benefit compensations. The demonstration resulted in a $350,000 in state funds for retraining programs and extension of important workers' rights and benefits for those Chinese workers who used to work in the largest garment plant in Northville. This type of community work produces a sense of accomplishments and results not only for the women but also for the community. There are many community workers like Emily who has touched my life and my work. They have left a deep impression on me as a researcher and a participant in that community. The work they do in and for the community had shattered my previous perception of minority people and their communities in that they cannot simply be known as a cultural entity or group that is deprived and dominated in a white society. They have given me a new-found knowledge.

Community work is seen here as a form of resistance to cultural and economic assaults and as an essential tool to the maintenance and survival of the community. This study provides evidence that women's public participation in the community is political in that they mobilize themselves to set goals, implement actions and accomplish results in planning for the community. In addition, their participation has a historical precedent in that Chinese women have participated actively since

the 1940's. Even though the Chinese community's development in the United States
has been shaped and controlled historically by outside forces, the community has not
remained passive. This study provides a new perspective in using women's community
work to look at organized resistance strategies that affect political realities and
development in the Chinese community today.

I would like to thank my professors who have been supportive and critical toward
the development of this work. They include Dr. Evelyn S.N. Glenn, my mentor; Dr. Sally
W. Cassidy, Dr. Paule Verdet, Dr. Peter Langer and Dr. Cheryl T. Gilkes. I would
also like to thank Dr. Robert J. Theodoratus for helping me publish this book.

My gratitude and heartfelt thanks go to the community workers in Northville Chinatown who made this research work a reality. To "Millie" who provided me the strategies in gaining access to become a community worker. And, to Ms. Anna Fang and my
husband, Peng-Khuan Chong for reading and editorial help.

INTRODUCTION

Very little is known in the sociological literature on Chinese Americans about the participation of Chinese women in the community. Community studies on Chinatown over the past twenty years tend to explain the emergence and maintenance of Chinatown as an isolated ethnic community and as a cultural phenomenon (Jacobs et al., 1971; Weiss, 1974; Lyman, 1974; Hsu, 1974). When the historical development of Chinese immigrants to the present time is traced in these studies, analyses are based on the subject of cultural and value conflicts between the young and the old (Lyman, 1974; Sung, 1971; Weiss, 1974).[1] No studies contribute a detailed picture of the Chinese women in either American society or the Chinese-American community. Moreover, when women are discussed in these studies it is often a minor aspect to the overall view of the community. Lyman (1974:86-116) describes the arrival of women immigrants to the United States and how their arrival created a family-based community that replaced the structure of the pre-World War II community, but does not mention their role again.

Even in studies of the family, women are not discussed directly. Haynor (1930: 908-11) points out that the familial system has supressed juvenile delinquency in Chinatown, while Lee (1956) argues that the family structure produces cliquishness and prevents the Chinese from fully assimilating into American society. It is often understood but not mentioned in this literature that the Chinese-American woman's role is solely that of wife and mother. The critique by Lofland (1975:151) on community studies points out that the consequences of such community studies tend to direct researchers to empirical settings in which women are structurally and definitionally only "there," and moreover, treat women as "simply present." Such a narrow definition and parameter area in research on the Chinese community neglects an understanding of the Chinese women who have moved beyond the familial boundaries to the public spheres of the community and working environment.

1

Demographic studies offer another view of Chinese women: that many are working in the labor force. Sung's (1976) study of the 1970 census on women found that 49.5% of the Chinese females in the United States work full-time as compared to 43.4% white and 47.5% black women who are in the labor force. Moreover, 19.4% of these Chinese women hold professional and technical positions as compared to 15.9% of the white women. 3.8% of the Chinese women are employed as managers and administrators, which is similar to the percentage of white women in these positions.[2] However, these demographic studies do not explain much about the lives of these women, their class backgrounds, or their problems in the white society.

The rise of the Asian-American movement on major college campuses in the 1970's created a whole area of research in the forms of short articles that are gender-based. However, this literature focuses on consciousness-raising ideas for discussing women's position under racism, such as Payton-Miyasaki's (1971:117) article that raises the question of traditional ethnic values in the following way:

> Even though Western women are deprived of participation in the mainstream of their culture, we Asian women are far more deprived of opportunities and learnings than Western women.

Consciousness-raising literature is a step forward in focusing on the problems of Asian women. It is useful in analysis of self-identity and discussion of personal conflict experienced in the white society. It is fruitful especially in consciousness-raising groups such as the ones that I have participated in. However, such studies do not provide a concrete analysis of the survival strategy which women use or can use to combat the racism that is discussed at length in this literature. Moreover, by categorizing Chinese women simply into an Asian-American group, specific cultural, historical, social and behavioral differences are ignored. Asians include Indians, Chinese, Malays, Koreans, Japanese, Vietnamese, Thais, Cambodians and Filipinos; and each ethnic group emerges out of a unique set of historical situations. Each ethnic group's status in relation to the society, to their culture and to their community tends to be lost in

2

such a generalization. Finally, and most importantly, these studies outline problems
and conditions that are produced by racism, particularly stereotyping and loss of identity, and lack the theoretical approach that serves as an important tool in providing
a research framework to the study of women, and in my case, the research on Chinese
women and their involvement in Chinatown.[3]

I view the Chinese community as an internal colonial enclave. Since there is an
absence of Chinatown studies that draws upon the internal colonialism model (Hirata,
1976:24)[4], this chapter will introduce the theoretical concepts that underlie the
approach of viewing community work as necessary to maintain and ensure the survival
of the community.

Colonialism refers to the "establishment of domination over a geographical external political unit, most often inhabited by people of a different race and culture,
where this domination is political and economic, and the colony exists subordinated
to and dependent upon the mother country" (Blauner, 1972:83). The concept of colonialism has been extended to refer also to enclaves within a developed region. The
internal colony differs in that the geographical distance is absent, and the ethnic
group is subjected to the domination of the "host" society. The feature characteristics of a colonial enclave include indirect political and economic controls by the
white society. Most important, the enclave is dependent economically and politically
on the larger society. However, the central characteristic, as Mina Caulfield (1972:
189) has pointed out, is that:

> ...key decisions on the disposition of resources and benefits
> in a community are made by members of another ethnic or cul-
> tural group.

In order for such decisions to be made, the significant process of colonization weakens individual and collective will to resisting oppression (Blauner, 1972:90). It is
not difficult to contain and control the Chinese community, as the traditional leadership - the pro-Taiwan Chinese Consolidated Benevolent Association (CCBA) is based on

the gaining of wealth and prestige by the merchants and not the community; moreover, the leadership that maintains the status quo further exploits the masses in their own group by continually supplying and managing the cheap Chinese labor force as well as keeping their wages down. The colonizers have always treated the Chinese as an out-side group in the United States. The endless restriction acts or exclusion laws pass-ed in the period from 1785 to 1920[5] clearly indicated that Chinese-Americans were viewed as an "undesirable group." Recent means of controlling the Chinese population have extended to limiting the number of Chinese immigrants under a strict immigration quota system as well as likely eliminating the Fifth Preference that affects family reunification of siblings of U.S. citizens.[6]

The colonial relationship with its enclave is based upon economic exploitation of their land, labor and resources. Chinese laborers in this country were recruited in the nineteenth century to work in the railroad and gold mining industries. Their job conditions were considered degrading by American laborers: low-pay, high risk and entailing long hours (Bonacich, 1979:27). Other jobs were not opened to them. Today, jobs situated in the Chinese enclave still conform to these conditions and standards, especially in the Chinese restaurants, hotels and garment factories. Long excluded from unions, Chinese workers in Chinatown are unable to organize and improve their conditions. The community enclave's structure produces and maintains an exploitation of the Chinese workers. Recent Chinese immigrants because of their inability to speak English are trapped into the subeconomy, forced to work for low wages, live in sub-standard tenements, and maintain a standard of living below the poverty level. This is still a common phenomenon in major Chinatowns throughout the United States (Light and Wong, 1975).

Secondly, under the impact of colonization, the Chinese culture and social organi-zation cannot be completely reconstructed in a new environment. The Exclusion Act of 1882 compelled men to marry in Kwantung and commute back and forth to visit their

4

wives and it was not only in the 1920's that a Chinese family could be reconstructed in the "host" society (Nee and Nee, 1974:148). Interracial marriage was forbidden and, according to federal law, a woman who entered into such a marriage automatically lost her citizenship in the United States, even if she was a citizen by birth. This imposition on intermarriages was not repealed until the 1940's (Huange, 1954:178-180).

Cultural assaults under the colonial rule constrain, transform or destroy indigenous values, orientations and ways of life of the Chinese people in this country. Family lifestyle is affected tremendously.[7] The continual exploitation of Chinese women in porno-films, and in the American entertainment media completely distort the true and realistic picture of Chinese-American women in this country. These films still reinforce the stereotypes of Chinese women as exotic, demure, quiet and non-obstrusive. Food also underwent cultural distortion in the new environment. Food like chop-suey and fortune cookies do not exist in restaurants in Asia, but they are considered Chinese here in America. The festival celebrations also lose their traditional forms when they are restructured here, their meanings and symbols fading with each passing generation.

In looking at the Chinese community through internal colonialism model, one should not view this as an acceptance of the historical situations and treatment imposed by the colonizers, but as a perspective to provide an important analysis that is often lacking in other theoretical approaches to looking at the historical processes that lead to movements of separatism, cultural nationalism and struggles of national liberation as forms of political action. As Hirata (1976:24) points out, the internal colonialism perspective differs from the institutional racism model in that it does not end with institutional reform, but pushes towards a more fundamental change of the social system which will allow for the self-determination of minority people. This study is a focus on community work as a form of resistance and struggle to maintain and enable the survival of the community. The study maintains that the role women

5

play in the community is inherently political; for the women organize themselves to change a particular course in the community by setting up goals, implementing certain actions and accomplishing results in their planning for the community.

Forms of resistance have been common in colonization history. The colonial enclave is not a passive and docile entity. The so-called riots are organized as one form of mass rebellion against colonial status (Blauner, 1972:89). Other forms of strategies that have been adopted are the famous women's revolt in the Ibo region of Nigeria in 1929, hunger strikes of Gandhi in the colonial days in India and recently in Ireland, sit-ins by American blacks in the Civil Rights Movement, and boycotts in the recent busing situation in the Chinese community in Northville. Other forms of cultural resistance can be found for instance, in the family sphere in the Appalachian region, where:

> Mountain children are taught early to act proper in public and hillbilly at home...how to use the stereotype for protection and to confound, aggravate, harass and thwart the colonizer....One example is the stereotype of laziness, dependency and irresponsibility which the Appalachian has learned to effectively manipulate to sabotage the colonizer's attempts to organize the mountaineer into pseudo-participatory democracy rituals which further splinter Appalachian solidarity (Lewis et al., 1973:151 also in Caulfield, 1974:81).

Community work, too, can be seen as a form of resistance in maintaining and consolidating the community. It is an attempt by Chinese Americans to organize; change and improve the conditions and problems of the community under colonization; and collectively respond and strategize against further oppression.

Community workers dedicate their skills and efforts to the community as part of a larger network of community activists who belong to both old and new organizations established in the Chinese community. These associations help to dispense job opportunities, social services and recreation as well as handle issues for the people in the community. Members of the community organization have played and continue to play a major role in uniting the people in times of trouble and helping to organize

6

strategies for both survival and change in the community. The majority of these workers are Chinese women, young and old, that come from all parts of the city, community,
and suburbs and have devoted themselves for a considerable time. They bring with them
resources, expertise and strength to serve and improve the Chinese community.

The following study introduces a community in the northeast region of the United
States. I called this Chinese community, Northville Chinatown. I spent more than a
year there as a researcher interviewing, attending workshops and meetings of organizations; and also become a community worker, helping the agencies and the people in
the community. The materials I gathered for this study and the experiences I had in
Northville Chinatown are enriching as well as overwhelming in learning first-hand
about the Chinese community and its relationship to the greater part of the American
society. This research is only a beginning in looking at women's participation and
activism in the Chinese community and I hope that others may continue to pursue this
interest in further detail than I have produced.

CHAPTER I   NORTHVILLE CHINATOWN

Northville is a city located in the northeast region of the United States. The
first Chinese who came to the city in the 1870's were laborers recruited to work in
the construction and manufacturing industries.[1] Because of the transient nature of
their work the early Chinese settlers stayed close to the railroad station of the city.
As the immigrants increased in numbers in the late 1800's, the Chinese settlers began
to take over the present Chinatown area that was successively occupied by the Irish,
Italians and Syrians.[2] One community worker told me, her late father told her that
in those early days, the community was relatively small and it was comprised of two
main streets: B Street and Ox Street in Northville (see Figure 2, on page 9). While
she was growing up in the 1920's, Chinatown was still small and families and friends
knew each other well. After 1945, the population in Northville Chinatown began to
grow at a fast rate and by 1950, the Chinese population in the area reached 1,600.[3]

It is important to note that the Chinese Exclusion Act of 1882 played a large role
in preventing Chinese women from coming to the United States. Thus, the community was
essentially a workingman neighborhood with little or no family life (Lyman, 1974:87).
The immigration laws were relaxed after the postwar (World War II) period,[4] this
affected the entry of brides, refugees, displaced persons, and professionals into the
city and the neighborhood underwent a substantial change from a bachelor society to
a family group neighborhood. Today, the ratio of men to women is almost equal.[5]

This chapter provides an overview of Northville Chinatown; the Chinese people in
the community and their problems; and the crises and conditions that are unique to
this particular neighborhood. The following topics are addressed: population growth
and land encroachment, housing, dialect and class divisions, employment, the position
of women in the community, the family, the Chinese youth, elderly in the community,
and Chinatown as an internal colony.

8

Figure 1 Map of Northville Chinatown

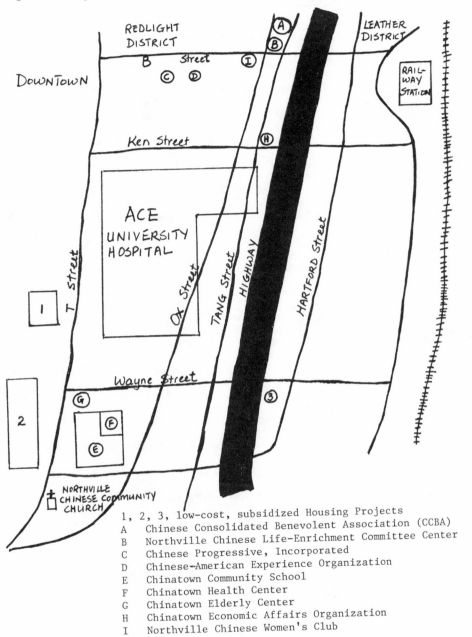

1, 2, 3, low-cost, subsidized Housing Projects
A   Chinese Consolidated Benevolent Association (CCBA)
B   Northville Chinese Life-Enrichment Committee Center
C   Chinese Progressive, Incorporated
D   Chinese-American Experience Organization
E   Chinatown Community School
F   Chinatown Health Center
G   Chinatown Elderly Center
H   Chinatown Economic Affairs Organization
I   Northville Chinese Women's Club

9

Population Growth and Land Encroachment

The urban renewal of Northville during the 1950's coincided with the influx of Chinese immigrants to the Chinatown area. Two major highways were built which removed almost 25% of the total land parcels in the community. Despite protest, many factories and families were relocated outside the area. And moreover, with the completion of the highway, traffic passing through the area caused pollution problems. Although there has been talk over the past ten years of building a park around Chinatown, it was not successful on two grounds: lack of financial support and lack of space. The discovery during the late 1950's that the Chinese community was sitting in the middle of the business district in Northville sent land prices soaring. The redevelopment plans of the city and land acquisition by a nearby educational institution, Ace University Hospital, shrunk the community in size. However, the population increase in the neighborhood never ceased. In the past ten years, the Chinese population in Northville Chinatown has grown by 25% to 5,000[6] in the southern side of the community.

Today, the community consists predominantly of working-class families and newly-arrived immigrants from Hong Kong, Taiwan, China and Indochina. As one walks in Chinatown, one only sees a few low-cost housing projects and deteriorating houses amidst the many restaurants and stores. Most of the middle-class Chinese move outside the community once they have saved enough money. Those who cannot afford to move and buy a car have to stay in an over-crowded polluted and congested area.

The changes that occurred over the past twenty-five years came rapidly. The high concentration of Chinese (43%) in this small area[7] has changed the once-small community to a cosmopolitan center for food, culture and business that not only attracts Chinese from outside this area but also others who frequent the nearby businesses and theater and red-light districts. The residents and community workers were struck by these social changes, especially when the 1980 census data were released and published

10

in the community newspaper, <u>Dragon Boat</u>, October 1982 issue. One community worker whom I showed the newspaper to commented:

> You know it's not just the fact that the numbers change so
> drastically. When I was growing up, we had 2,000 people.
> Everybody knew everybody and NOW [emphasis]....as I stand
> outside, I don't even know a soul that goes by [laugh].

The faces of the community are no longer recognizable by residents and less so are the visages of those who frequent the Chinatown area. I was most surprised to find a lot of new shops open in Northville while I was doing my fieldwork. When I commented on this to a woman who has lived here for almost fifty years, she shook her head and said sadly:

> I'm seeing more stores popping up everywhere near Chinatown,
> even on T Street opposite City Park where the rent is very high.
> I don't know how long these stores will survive, but you know,
> you've to open something to bring jobs to immigrants and relatives
> that are brought over from Asia.

The survival of shops in Northville Chinatown is extremely difficult. The restaurant industry has reached a plateau point in developing its own resources. Space is very scarce and for those restaurants opened outside the core area of the business district the rent is extremely high. According to a businessman who owned some property in Chinatown, fifteen dollars per square foot is the market price for a business office space and it would not be surprising for rent to go up to five thousand or more per month. It requires a lot of capital to keep a restaurant afloat. In Northville, one of the highest cost-of-living areas in the country, to maintain a small business without outside help (such as the Small Business Administration) and maintain a break-even at the start of the venture is almost an impossibility. The risk especially is high in a period when the economy is still in a recession.

Housing in Chinatown

The rapid changes of Chinatown occur not only in this community but also in other communities in Northville. Like other cities, Northville was urbanized early in the twentieth century. Its growth and urbanization like that of other major cities in the United States was not a planned process. Growth not only brought profits and capital to the city but also social problems that could not be solved overnight. A study on city urbanization in the United States revealed a list of 123 "distressed" cities of which eighty-three are situated in the northeast (Nathan and Dommel, 1977). These cities suffer mostly from a high unemployment rate, aging dilapidated housing, poverty, crime, traffic congestion, loss of taxpayers - both individual and corporate, and the loss of essential services. Third-world minority communities within these cities are hit the hardest. A study (ANCD, 1971:i) on Northville Chinatown, published eleven years ago, also calls attention to the above-mentioned problems but what strikes the reader in this study is the opening statement:

> Conditions among Northville's Chinese, one of the city's
> oldest but least known communities, are in many respects
> worse than among any other groups.

The report also revealed that since Chinatown was situated in the oldest part of the city, over 72% of the housing was deteriorated as compared to only 14% of the city. Moreover, Northville Chinatown is over-crowded; the report rated over 75% as compared to the city's figure of only 7.7% (pp. i-ii). These conditions are a major concern for the residents and the community workers and it has always been the first priority for them.

The housing situation has remained the same since it was first built by the original occupants in the 1860's.[8] According to a woman activist, large buildings that are rented out to the Chinese tenants in Chinatown are owned by white landlords, while small buildings are occupied by the Chinese owners themselves. However, the overall

12

maintenance of housing in Chinatown remains poor. Rent is expensive: a studio apartment is $300 per month, a one-bedroom is $400 per month, and a two-bedroom is $500 per month.[9] However, the landlords do not maintain the housing, and in many cases when housing proves to be a losing venture, the landlords will sell the buildings to interested outside parties since land value in this area has increased over the past thirty years. Even though rent has increased, the tenants in this area remain since, as immigrants, they cannot afford to move to a better neighborhood. But the over-crowded conditions and the lack of plumbing are not healthy to the individuals that live here. Moreover, when the tenants are evicted, they are given short notice to move out. Tenants that live here feel that they are powerless because they lack information about resources and professional legal advice to fight for their rights. There is a long waiting list for low-cost housing established in the 1970's that is subsidized. A community worker and resident in the community told me that would-be residents have to wait for at least three to five years. Yet, housing subsidies are running out and there is a fear in the community that they will no longer be able to afford the high cost of housing in the future.

The land takeover by outside groups is another cause for concern. The community residents see the community shrinking. Many residents and workers were displaced by the gradual takeover of the city in the name of redevelopment as well as by the expansion of Ace University Hospital in the center of Chinatown. Such a gradual encroachment on a neighborhood can be very destructive not only to the residents that live there but also to a long-preserved culture and to the jobs necessary to the poor, working-class individuals for their survival.

Gans' (1962:303-304) study of the destruction of the West End in Boston is perhaps the best example of an ethnic neighborhood situated in a business district that was totally destroyed. The last days of the West End, where the Italian immigrants used to live, is best captured here in a passage of the city twenty years ago:

13

As buildings began to empty, the remaining tenants were loath to
remain in them, and even those who had planned to stay to the bitter
end began to leave...unknown teenagers began to roam through semi-
deserted buildings, using them for nocturnal parties, setting fires,
and vandalizing wherever they could. The families still remaining
in these buildings became fearful and moved more quickly than they
had intended. The empty structures were torn down as soon as the
last tenant left, and the resulting noise and dirt encouraged
people in adjacent buildings to move also. Consequently, the West
End was emptied in little more than eighteen months after the official taking of the land.

Scattered locations being taken by outside groups can easily destroy a shrinking com-

munity. The West Enders were given only eighteen months' notice by the city to va-

cate the area. It was scant time for preparation and to organize the residents to-

gether to fight against the city. Also, they lacked mobilizing experience. What

happened to the West End also had happened to many Chinatowns in cities such as New

York, or Montreal, Canada where large parcels of land were taken away. These threat-

ening pictures of redevelopment are frightening ones for immigrants who are setting up

homes in the city. That large parcels of nearby areas in Northville Chinatown are

being zoned for the future expansion of hotels and shops has recently become known to

the Chinese in Northville. In addition, the nearby theater developments as well as

the university expansion all present an urgent challenge for the community to act

immediately on these concerns.

Dialect and Class Divisions

Apart from the physical and environmental changes in the community, internal

changes are also felt. One of the major changes in the composition of the popula-

tion is caused by successive waves of immigrants from different parts of China

that move into the community. Before the influx of immigrants in the late 1950's

and 1960's, the Northville Chinese came largely from Toisan which is a district

in Kwantung Province in the southeast region of China. Their special dialect,

Toisanese, is very different from the Cantonese dialect of the Chinese immigrants

14

of the late 50's and 60's from Hong Kong. One who speaks fluent Cantonese cannot understand or speak Toisanese easily. Today, the immigrants that come from Asia speak so many different dialects that Mandarin is used as a common language. The influx of the Indochinese immigrants into this area in the 1970's also brought changes into the community. One resident whom I have interviewed told how she sees such differences and their impact on the community:

> When I first live here as a teenager, most people were Chinese, most people speak Toisanese rather than Cantonese; and as the years go by, there are more Hong Kong people...there are more refugees, the type of people who live in Chinatown is different now and the purpose to provide, you know has changed...

Such changes that occurred in recent years have caused tremendous concern and sometimes the differences of dialect have caused rifts and resentment among members of the community.

Workers in the Community

In Chinatown today, the immigrants no longer are employed in the construction and manufacturing industries as were the immigrants first recruited here a century ago. The majority of men and women find jobs in the restaurants and garment industries that are not only in Chinatown, but also in the suburbs in Northville. Some Chinese restaurant workers travel as far as across state lines to work in restaurants. These jobs involve low pay and long hours. Little English is demanded or learned by Chinese people employed in these industries, and the long hours and arduous conditions leave little time for employees to learn or take classes for their own advancement. Family members working at different restaurants and factory shifts rarely see each other and are seldom together on weekends due to the struggle to survive. They rarely have the opportunity to adjust to the new American way of life since most start their life and work in Chinatown.

The garment factories that Chinese women work in are not unionized and there are
few benefits such as medical insurance, vacation pay, and seniority pensions given to
workers. Many who came to Northville feel that life here is not what they came to expect from the movies they saw in the East, or the talk of friends who came to visit
them. There is upward mobility, but their opportunities are few because they lack
language proficiency in English and few have a good education and qualification.
Teenagers especially are often caught in low-paying restaurant jobs with little advancement, yet they cannot participate in other job training programs provided by the
city for those who lack English language skills. While I was handling a court case
as a translator in Northville, I met five teenagers ranging from sixteen to seventeen
years old. They did not know English, even though they had been here for a couple of
years, and they still worked in restaurants. I also met an older male who said that
he had been here for ten years. He spoke English haltingly and understood conversation but since he had no opportunity to read and write he had remained in the restaurant job for ten years since he came from Asia.

The Chinese Women in the Community

Women who live in the community bear a tremendous burden in taking care of their
children and maintaining a household. While the extended family household is common
in China, this is not so in Northville Chinatown. Angie, a social worker who does
outreach in Chinatown through the health center, told me that the majority of Chinese
women who came to Northville are brought over by their husbands. They come here to
get married and do not bring their parents or family with them. Once they settle
down to married life here, they immediately have children and work at the same time
in the garment factories. Because the family is nuclear, these women are unable to
find outside help when they are working; and in Chinatown today, there is only one
day-care center that takes only seventy children.

16

In and adjacent to Chinatown, there are forty-seven garment companies that employ 47% (2,162) Asian women, the majority of whom working there are Chinese.[10] These women work long hours, sometimes involving overtime to supplement their family income. Their lives are hard, according to Angie who does outreach in Chinatown to recruit these women to her program. She told me that single men often go back to Hong Kong to get married and do not know their brides long enough when they bring them back to the States. Fear that their wives will run away after they are here motivates men to want children immediately once they return to America. Once the children have arrived, the women spend the rest of their lives working, and looking after the children; which leaves them with no time to know the area they have come to stay in and to enjoy a few social activities. This happened to one of the women that was interviewed. The housewife came to Northville three years ago and was in a typical situation for immigrant wives here in the community. She recounted her life in the following way:

> My husband went to Hong Kong to marry me. At that time I thought
> America must be really nice. I came back with him. I know my
> husband for a very short time....
> There are little social activities here. Most of my friends I know
> play mahjong. One has to endure so much here to carry on a marriage
> ....But, before I got married in Hong Kong, I never would have
> thought that life would be so hard.
> In Hong Kong, I watched a lot of American TV series, and I thought
> that everyone's houses are so beautiful, even the firemen's!! I
> always thought that in America, the food and the clothes you buy
> are the best. After I arrived, what I have seen here made me very
> upset....Even when you learn to speak English, life hasn't change
> for the better....If I would have my life all over again, I wouldn't[11]
> come here in the first place....

Many women have made the same mistake and cannot help but feel disillusioned. The media is one of the means by which many Chinese women and men today learn about the "American way of life." However, they only glimpse the image of middle-class America and do not realize that the stories and scenes are selective to attract public viewing. For those who have never been to America, it is difficult to know what is the reality of American life until they experience it personally, and then it may be a little too late. In Northville Chinatown there are more divorces than many Chinese would

17

believe. While doing my translator's job I was told that many cases in court are marital ones. The Chinese family structure today is very fragile especially for the working class who have a hasty marriage arrangement.

The Chinese Family in Chinatown

The lack of social support is very difficult not only for women in the community but also for the family as a whole. Often the husbands have to work late at night and on weekends. Ann, a volunteer community worker who has dealt with marital conflicts and parental issues for many years told me:

> ...the family structure still stay where it was: the sophistication isn't there yet, the interpersonal relationship between two members, particularly between two-generational members still remain pretty much the same.....I don't know whether they can get into the level that the American society has where the father and son are like friends, patting each other's shoulders and go out together. I don't know when is that going to happen. Hopefully it's going to be soon.
> I still see that mothers still dominate the day-to-day operations in the family, the father is somewhere....[pause for a long time, with a faraway look on her face].

Not only is there a lack of social and family support from the spouse, but also from neighbors and friends. Even though living in the same neighborhood, the women do not know each other well since there is little time for them to socialize outside the family and work environment. The neighbors also work full-time and are not accessible when the women need them. The situation is becoming worse. Lynn, a community worker who does outreach program, told me her own experience of dealing with parents whom she has come to know:

> You see more women running away when they could not deal with the situation...because you don't have the relatives and closer family here in this country; the support system you know to keep the family together and I see more families breaking up now...

It is difficult to learn more about women's lives in the community. The community workers come to know most women through their work organizing parents, or as fellow enants in the neighborhood, and most have encountered the same problems that women

ave to face in their day-to-day lives in Northville Chinatown.

The Chinese Youth

Today in Northville, more than one-fourth of the population (28%) consists of

oung people under the age of eighteen. 74% of this group is attending public school

n Northville. Children who live in the community are exceptional in that teachers

hat I have talked to say that most Chinese children learn at a very young age to be

ndependent and to take care of themselves. This is because both of the parents work

nd it is not rare for children to come home to an empty apartment. The children

arely see their fathers because of their fathers' restaurant jobs. The fathers come

ome after 10:00 or 11:00 p.m., often work on weekends as well. Children have to cope

ith the outside world by themselves, since English is not usually spoken at home.

'requently, children are confronted with two different sets of rules: what they learn

n school about the American way of life and what they learn from their parents about

he Chinese way of life. Since a child will spend most of his or her life in the

ommunity, he or she has no opportunity to learn more about American society. Nettie,

 social worker who works with children in Chinatown told me what she has observed in

er work:

> Growing up in Chinatown, you [the child] feel less secured,
> you have very little contact with people outside the commu-
> nity and they don't have the skills...either social or ver-
> bal to relate to people outside the community when they go
> out to work. They will face problems. They're shy and
> when they grow up, they really have a hard time sometimes
> fighting for their own rights

'arents, or the first-generation Chinese who came here, generally do not understand

 lot of English. They are not familiar with the American public school system and

ost of the time do not know what their children are going through. Thus, poor com-

unication between parents and children often occurs in such an environment. In

19

today's Chinatown, delinquency is on the rise. Street fights and gang killings, once never heard of, begin to be a fact of life in the community. I have worked with young adults in court in Northville as a translator, a position which allowed me a glimpse into the life of these delinquents in the community. Because of my delicate involvement with the court, abiding by the rules and regulations of privacy, I can only reveal some parts of my experiences and findings in this study.[12]

The Elderly in Chinatown

The elderly population is the first generation of a wave of Chinese Americans who came here before the war brides, students and recent immigrants from Asia. The first wave of Chinese came here as sojourners to work on railroad, in gold mines and construction and manufacturing industries. The elderly Chinese face tremendous changes in a community with little social support. Isolation, high rent, fear of eviction, and overcrowding are some problems that they must deal with. The elderly were unable to vote or exert any but the most marginal political influence until 1952 when they became citizens in this country. Because of their alienated existence and fear of deportation, they are reluctant to become involved with legal and business issues and seek medical care, legal advice, or financial help until their difficulties have reached an extreme stage (Kalish and Moriwaki, 1973:203). They can be considered a silent subgroup that is often overlooked by society at large, and often they are not included in aid given to the elderly population of this country. According to a report on the White House Conference on Aging in 1971, their silence results in the "....myth that pervades society at large and permeates the policy decisions of agencies and governmental entities...that Asian-American aged do not have any problems, that Asian Americans are able to take care of their own, and that Asian-American aged do not need or desire aid in any form" (The Asian American Elderly, 1972:2). Such a myth distorts the reality Chinese elderly face in this country.

20

Most of them spent their lives living and working within the community and lacked opportunities to learn and acquire sufficient language skills to survive outside the community. The government-subsidized housing and medical programs for the general elderly population do not benefit the Chinese elderly group because the elderly population rarely seek outside assistance. This is due partly to the fact that they lack the knowledge and relevant information and because outside agencies have never done outreach work in the community. In Chinatown, 11.2% of the total Chinese population are elderly (65 years and over). This is similar to Northville's total elderly population (12.56%) and is considered high in the Chinese community.

The elderly need constant medical attention, yet medical care rarely reaches this population group because of poverty and language handicaps that prevail. Chinese, especially the older generation, view sickness differently than people from Western cultures. A routine treatment procedure for Western doctors may conflict in some instances with the practices of Chinese medicine, where forces of nature are seen to have a great relation to the healing or treatment process.[13] Recognition of the cultural and social practices of the elderly is an important consideration in providing and improving care and services suitable to the needs of this population.

The current crisis that the community faces today is exacerbated by Reagan's policy and budget cuts. The closing of Little City Hall, cancellations of programs, and reduction of funds are the main concerns of the Chinese community. At the same time, the new influx of Indochinese immigrants have taxed the community's strength and resources for survival. These are problems that community workers have to deal with. Through their work they perceive a community that is constantly struggling to survive, and to change and to improve. Their struggle is a constant response to the external and internal social forces that affect the community. Northville Chinatown may appear like other Chinese communities in the United States, but the similarity lies only in certain common external forces that affect them.

21

Chinatown as a Community Enclave

Whether in Northville or any other American city, the Chinese community today is a product of racial oppression. The Chinese people have been explicitly targeted in the past as an ethnic group that does not belong in America. An examination of the anti-Chinese movement in American history is necessary to an understanding of the social characteristics and conditions that prevail in the Chinese community. The Chinese do not have a choice to participate equally in the life and culture of American society. They are still not being fully accepted in the society as an assimilated or semi-assimilated minority group, and their needs have been neglected for a long time. The 1971 study in Northville Chinatown (ANCD, 1971:83) revealed the following relevant information on the city's relationship to the minority community of Chinatown:

> Chinatown, despite its many problems currently receives little aid from Northville area institutions. The community, in need of housing and physical improvements, has been largely denied the necessary public investment. The social service needs of Chinatown have not been met by City agencies.

It is said that in the 1960's, minorities progressed further than in any other period in American history, especially because of the poverty campaign for minority and third-world communities. This report, based on the 1970 census information, however, does not reveal any aids that the Chinese community receives from the outside. This lack of support is especially difficult for the community and its people in this present ecnomic recession. Yet even in prosperous times, minority communities remain neglected.

The Chinese community is not only a product of racial oppression but also is a product of colonization. The Chinese community is an internal colony within American society whose productive system inside the colonial enclave is dependent and controlle nationally. As Stanford Lyman (1974:29) points out, "The relationship between ghetto community and metropolitan authorities bears a close resemblance to that which

22

revailed in the British, Dutch, and French colonies in Oceania and Southeast Asia."
o put it explicitly, Chinatown's economic development is shaped by its dependent re-
ation to the dominant society. Their capital-goods or service-good production sec-
ors are not strong enough to develop independently of outside influence. The enclave
lays the "interdependency" game that is exemplified by many colonized and developing
ountries in the world.[14]

One such dependent industry, an economic mainstay of American Chinatowns since
920, is the tourist industry. The industry is comprised of restaurants, curio stores,
mport bazaars, groceries, fish and meat markets, and side-walk stalls (Light and Wong,
975). The tourists are vital to the survival of the community and its economy. In
uch a relationship the community has to rely on outside forces to give life to its
conomy.

The second example of development in the colonial enclave under American capital-
stic expansion is the invested capital on the redevelopment project, the Lantern
quare, in Northville Chinatown. Plans are underway to build a hotel, convention and
hopping center with the Chinese minorities playing a large role in bringing curio
tores, restaurants and entertainment to the large buildings. Such a capital invest-
ent project, to be completed in the end of 1990, could not originate from the Chi-
ese themselves, but from the external government forces. The land and profit value
n this area will increase due to the exploitation of a cheap and easily-supplied lo-
al labor force. However, the re-invested capital and large yield in profit ulti-
ately benefit the government and institutions in the city. In other words, the ex-
ernal forces control the economy of Chinatown.

Service organizations from the 1970's somewhat improved the situation in China-
own, but these improvements have been slight and in poor economic times are substan-
ially reduced. Moreover, when there are results, these tend to be minor and basi-
ally the community remains as it is, with the same problems, same conditions, and

23

the same poor immigrants. Blauner (1972:40) explains his view of colonized minority

groups:

> Improvements in income and occupation are not easily translated
> into an overall raising of social status and increase in politi-
> cal effectiveness, as they are for white groups. The symbols
> and prerequisites by which status is validated - improved resi-
> dence, neighborhood, and life style - are not available.

This is a reality that a community like Northville Chinatown has to deal with.

Thus, community work is necessary and critical to the survival of the community. The

emergence of such community work arises out of the concern for the neglected social

problems that plague the community. It is a form of resistance, which men and women

engage in, to maintain, support and improve the community's situation for a better

tomorrow.

CHAPTER II   THE EMERGENCE OF COMMUNITY WORK

It is important in the study of community workers to first comprehend the histo-
ical development of the community so as to see the types of community work that
merged in response to the need of the overall community. This chapter traces the
istorical development of community work and women's involvement in Northville China-
own.

The development of community work occurred essentially in three stages: the
ioneering stage that began in the 1940's, the professional stage that began in the
ate 1960's and the activist stage that began in the mid-1970's. The chart (figure
hree, page 26) illustrates the types of women at work, their orientation, and the
inkage or the alliances made at that particular period with organizations or coun-
ries outside of Northville Chinatown. The chart is partly self-explanatory and can
e referred back to as the following pages unfold the historical development of the
ommunity work that is a part of the development of Northville Chinatown. Although
here is a beginning for all organizations and for all community workers, there is no
xplicit ending because the clubs, churches, and organizations exist as part of
orthville Chinatown, and the ranks of professional, official, and activist community
orkers are constantly rejuvenated by new community workers (new blood). The workers
nd oganizations exist together in a world of change, encounters and experiences.

The Pioneering Stage

The Chinese have always looked toward their community as a place of warmth,
shelter, familiarity and culture. The new immigrants in this country gravitate toward the city's Chinatown where the place and people look more like "home" than a
foreign land. The community, with its small and centralized space, is able to help

25

Figure 2 Historical Development of Community Work in Northville Chinatown

Stages	Types of Community Workers	Orientations	Linkages & Alliances
Stage I: Pioneering (1940's)	Club & Church women (pioneers), mostly retired now	− Exclusive members only − Patriotic China-related political & support work, charity work − Other activities include social & cultural events	Motherland: China (pre-revolutionary), Republic of China, Kuo Ming Tung (KMT) Party
Stage II: Professional (late 1960's)	Volunteers, professionals, officials, with some activists after mid-1970's	− Exclusive members only − Service-oriented; such as health, education, economy & business, youth & drugs, housing, welfare	U.S. Government, state & city agencies
Stage III: Activist (mid-1970's)	Students, professionals, political organizers, community people	− Membership opened to ALL − Issue-oriented; such as housing, education, equality & opportunity − Grassroot, people-solving − Other activities include social, cultural & recreational events	People's Republic of China, Asian-American Movement, third-world groups & organizations

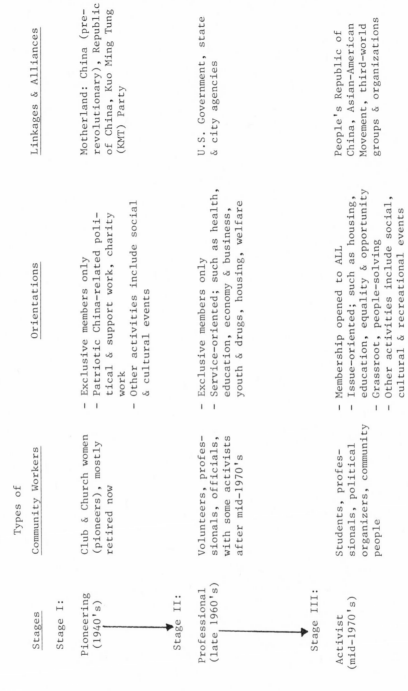

untrymen in need. It is a place where one can make friends, speak the dialect with-
it any trouble, find food and, most of all, the culture to ease the fear of being in
strange land.

Family associations or clans, formed in the 1890's when the Chinese began to
ettle in Northville, take care of the major social and financial needs of the immi-
rants who came to America. Family associations were established to assume a number
f responsibilities and duties to members with the same surname.[1] They organized
rotherhoods in trade, manufacturing, and types of labor, and provided mutual aid and
ssistance to young and retired members within the same group. For example, in San
rancisco, the Dear clan tended to operate the fruit and candy stores, and the Yee
nd Lee clans owned better-class restaurants and supplied most of the cooks in domes-
ic service (Lyman, 1974:30-32). Such help was basic in that it served the male
aborers and merchants who were the groups that established the community in North-
ille.

The increasing members of clans in the Chinese community gradually caused a cer-
ain degree of competition and rivalry in staking out their particular territory or
ype of business trade in a small community area (Kwong, 1979:41). In order to
inimize the kind of chronic disunity in the community, an umbrella agency called
he Chinese Consolidated Benevolent Association (CCBA) was set up in the 1900's
o incorporate all these family associations and community groups in Northville
hinatown as well as in other Chinatowns. The primary concern of CCBA is to oversee
usiness transactions; and to regulate labor, commerce, debt-collection, resource
llocation, dispute-settling and protection in the community (ANCD, 1971; Jacobs et
l., 1971; Nee and Nee, 1971; Lyman, 1974; Weiss, 1974; Kwong, 1979; Thompson, 1979).
n Northville, the CCBA currently is comprised of eleven representatives from
ifferent organizations that sit on its board,[2] and it claims to be the only commu-
ity spokesperson and official voice of Northville Chinatown.

27

As immigration restrictions were relaxed after World War II, the gradual increase of new immigrants and increasing births among the Chinese began to change the composition of the population in Chinatown. The new immigrants are largely from Hong Kong, where the main dialect spoken is Cantonese, and their cosmopolitan way of life differ greatly from the earlier Toisanese-dialect immigrants in Northville. The urban immigrants tend to ask their immediate family members for help rather than the family associations (Thompson, 1979). At the same time, the younger generation whether brought up in this country or in Asia cares very little about such affiliation with family associations. Educated and brought up in a working-class community, the majority of the young people tend to socialize more with their own peer group (Kendis and Kendis, 1976). They do not find any need to ally with the Kuo Ming Tung or Republic of China, as opposed to the earlier immigrants whose loyalty still lies with the Republic of China and believe it necessary that Chinese-Americans should always look towards the country as their motherland.[3]

As the population in Northville Chinatown increased in numbers, the community found itself unable to provide all the services needed by the new immigrants. Moreover, CCBA is not an agency that provides services to the individuals in the community even though it represents the people in Chinatown; its primary concern is in the area of economic and business transactions. Women community workers who remember the period before the great influx of immigrants into the community stated that the needs of community work were small-scale in nature. Community work was personalized and voluntary. There was no mass-scale organizing because the needs were covered by the community's family organizations and the Northville Chinese Community Catholic Church. Many women community workers worked in conjunction with the church. Jean, a community worker who sits on the board of Chinatown Economic Affairs told me about the community work her family did:

> Community work probably goes back to my mother; we used to bring
> old clothes to refugees from China. She was a very generous

person, she would give her clothes that she herself made and
would give to these refugees coming in....My mother [was]
formerly with the church....

One reason that community workers started getting involved in the community was to
give. They contributed individually to the people in need. The type of personalized
work ranged from giving away clothes to providing services that these women feel are
necessary for helping the immigrants individually. Mimi, a community worker who worked in the community for almost forty years, said that her work consisted of providing
individualized services whenever she was asked to do so, starting in the post-World
War II period. She said:

I do mostly social services for people like interpreting, translating, helping people to write letters and I'm very involved
in church work too. I feel that I've [got] to help because the
Lord sends us into this world to do a mission....

She finds that the community has changed so much now that community work provides for
much more than these little services for people.

The women's contribution[4] to community work and to the community is and has always
been visible. Women, especially Chinese women who came from a working-class background, have always coped with crises at home. However, their work is not limited to
just taking care of the house and their children. Sometimes, women who remember their
younger years said that helping their family business was necessary, and children were
brought up to help early in coping with their family situation. Women in the community were and are not secluded. Moreover, they are in touch with the reality of the
changing, problematic aspects of day-to-day survival of themselves and their community.

The earliest organization that was formed by Chinese women in Northville Chinatown
in 1940 was the Northville Chinese Women's Club that was led by Madam Soong Mei-Ling,
a member of a prominent KMT family who attended college here, and was active in political and social activities concerning Chinese women. Under the jurisdiction of the
CCBA, the Women's Club is a social as well as a political organization. At times, the
women also joined with the now-defunct Chinese Women's Patriotic Association in New

29

York's Chinatown in functions and activities that benefited the community.[5] Women

members in the Northville Chinese Women's Club were very active whenever a need arose

in the community. They also did much planning and political organizing for the commu-

nity. These zealous efforts that women expended in political work for support of

China during the World War II period was an important contribution that is not remem-

bered by many Chinese-American women today. A woman I talked to during a get-togethe

dinner told me, "Oh, ...everyone did that, I don't see it's any big thing." However,

the significance of such support work is part of the community work women do to main-

tain the national survival of all oppressed people, not only here in the community

but also in China.

Political work for support of China was considered crucial during the 1930's and

1940's when China was struggling to overthrow all foreign domination. The overseas

Chinese supported and contributed spiritually as well as financially to uniting China

Their concern stemmed from the overall treatment of Chinese in this country which is

always closely linked to the international standing of the homeland. Kwong (1979:93)

in examining the patriotic movement between 1904 and 1943 in New York's Chinatown

points out that the Chinese in this country have always attributed their mistreatment

here to their home government's weakness in the international arena, and the Chinese

believed they were discriminated against not out of some generalized antipathy toward

racial minorities but specifically because they were Chinese. Thus, for Chinese who

were in this country, fighting for China was an indirect means of fighting for them-

selves and their standing in the United States.

The concern for their people both here and in China prompted Chinese community

women such as the Women's Club in Northville to spend considerable time and effort to

do support work for their compatriots in China. I visited the Women's Club recently

and spent an entire Sunday afternoon with these women who were active during the war

period. These women showed their concern for China and its people by acting on what

30

hey all thought was necessary at the time. They did a lot of fund-raising and sales
f goods donated by local merchants. In addition, the women spent enormous time and
ffort to obtain clothes, food and medicine for refugees from China. Apart from these
olitical activities, they also organized social and cultural events like dance and
ong performances, Chinese movies and dinner parties. They raised money for other
ivic projects such as the cleaning and repairing of the gravestone for their members
n the cemetery. This is usually done every year of the Chinese Lunar calendar in
arch (which is April in the western calendar). Major preparations are made for the
ecessary repairs and their cost. According to Chinese custom, the Chinese devote one
articular day in March to bring flowers, food and fruits to the cemetery; sweep the
ravestones, and restore the surrounding grass of the plot of land. Usually this is
one by the deceased's family, however, when relatives were few in the United States,
omen in the club took over those duties.

Today, these women are no longer active for they lack the energy in recruiting new
embers or planning events. May Lee, a woman in her late sixties who held the presi-
ency of the club for a number of years, told me of the club's difficulties. She said
n Chinese:

> It's hard to organize now, for we are all getting too old,
> and so many of our members have passed away. Look at this
> place--it is in terrible shape and we have no money, we have
> no energy to raise money for upkeep of this place. It's
> really sad....Look at the New York women [meaning the Chinese
> Women's Patriotic Association in New York Chinatown], they've
> closed, do you know? Long time ago, but then...where are we
> now?

The club only opens its doors on weekends when members spend their leisure time tog-
ther playing mahjong and talking about old times. Most of these women are widowed,
and on the list of members that May Lee showed me only about one hundred members remained, whereas during the active period, the club had three hundred and fifty members.
These women have been here the greater part of their lives, and the club serves as
a place where they can maintain old friendships in the changing community environment.

31

The club women and church workers are the earliest women community workers to become active in the community. I called them "pioneer community workers" because they did not center their work only on their own clan and family associations' members, but emerged out of the traditional family organizations to do community work for all Chinese people, both within and outside of the Chinese community. However, their wor is not always visible to the public as compared to the present women community worker because the work they do is personalized, and only a small amount of time is spent on volunteer work. By that I mean voluntary positions require flexibility in time that these women may not always have, but they are not less regarded as not doing voluntee work, since it is understood among members that the women's main responsibilities are still the home and children. For those women who are willing to volunteer, large-scale organizing and planning is not required. These pioneer women workers concentrated their activities in the height of a crisis or an event. Once the crisis passed, the women devoted their time to other activities, often social, which were not considered a long-time contribution. However, when crises form an ongoing pattern, and when community issues remain unresolved, then community work is more visible to the public and its significance is appreciated by the people in the community.

The Professional Stage

The activities of women community workers became more visible as the community issues tended to become long-term. In the 1960's, the community began to feel that something must be done. The growth of social problems such as housing, education, the economic situation, and health could not be solved by a handful of individuals and church workers. The process of mobilizing the community started when Ace University Hospital began to encroach on the land adjacent to the community. Moreover, more immediate long-term plans by the university began to cause much concern among community workers. Recounting the beginning process of mobilizing the community, San-san, a

32

ommunity worker who is a bi-lingual teacher, told me what happened. She said:

> At that time, one of my friends...told me that Ace University was
> involved in the planning of a new school in Chinatown. Ace Univer-
> sity had not involved anyone from Chinatown in this planning and
> we decided this really wasn't right, I mean, this Ace University
> has never had any contact with the Chinese community, they don't
> hire people from the Chinese community an they were planning a
> school for us [laugh], that was absurd.
> So, we got involved, contacting people in the Chinatown area that
> would be affected....

he contacts that she and other community workers started set forward the process of

etting people who were concerned about the community involved in the land encroachment

ssues. Looking back, Katherine, a past official community worker told me:

> In a way, people don't realize it, but Ace was responsible
> for a lot of emerging organizations in the community be-
> cause a lot happened in reaction...on the actions that Ace
> has taken.

t was the concern that Ace University would dominate the community by not only taking

way its land but also in planning the community's need that prompted these women to

ecome involved in the community survival mission.

As community workers got involved with community problems, they found that the com-

unity as a whole lacked the strength and resources needed to deal with the on-going

ssues. First, they had no organization or source of funds. Second, they were inex-

perienced. Third, the problems that the Chinese community were facing were not known

to the public. A great deal of effort was spent in countless meetings to plan a large-

scale strategy to combat the neglect of problems in Chinatown. Katherine continued her

narration of their plan. She said:

> In 1969, a group of us got the Mayor and the city officials to
> come down to a public hearing in Chinatown and I would say that
> it probably is the first kind of social activism in Chinatown
> that was organized on a large scale.

The public hearing was the first that was ever planned in Chinatown. It provided an

opportunity for the community people and the city to meet and discuss the immediate

problems that Chinatown was facing. On the one hand, it was very successful as a first step toward identifying existing community problems. On the other hand, it als

brought out a lot of conflicts between the traditional and younger generations in the

community.

The successful organizing of the public hearing and conference was the first effo

by the developing community organizations toward coping with and improving the commun

ty situation. San-san told me:

> The public hearing addressed a few areas of concern. One of
> which has to do with...education, another had to do with cul-
> tural affairs, and public welfare in terms of sanitation. A
> fourth one has to do with health care which had already been
> identified with the Northville Chinese Life-Enrichment Commit-
> tee...

Overall, seven separate areas were discussed at length. They were: adult education,

economic development, education and day-care, health, physical development, church

affairs and social services.[6] Conference attendants were aware that the pioneering

stage of volunteer community work was no long effective. As the conference report

(NCLEC report, 1972:24) published by the Northville Chinese Life-Enrichment Commit-

tee points out:

> Dependence on volunteer help could not be viewed only as a
> stop-gap measure. Discussions and negotiation with potential
> funding sources must be done by a paid professional staff.

The community workers continued to meet after the public hearing in different task

forces that were set up according to problem areas.

The early 1970's was an important period in the community. A health center, eld-

erly center, community school, day-care center, youth services center, adult educatior

school and the Chinese Economic Affairs Organization were all established with funds

appropriated by the city, state and federal agencies. At the same time, Little City

Hall was also established in the community to provide a major link between the commu-

nity and the Mayor's Office. These organizations and their programs can be seen as

direct offsprings of federal programs and poverty campaign programs that were devel-

oped for minority communities during the late 1960's and early 1970's. To outsiders,

34

Chinatown is seen as an impoverished area in need of help. Many community workers who are facing cuts now remember how easy it was then to acquire the necessary funds in order to provide for the community services needed in Northville Chinatown.

Today, community workers, who talk about the success of establishing these social services and programs for the community people, still talk about the earlier organization, the Northville Chinese Life-Enrichment Committee (NCLEC) because the organization provided a success model and was the first agency to start some social services and programs in the community. A community worker described to me the significance of this agency first established in the late 1960's. Cleo said:

> The early NCLEC is a social club, and it provides civic activities which no one was doing, you know. The NCLEC is the GRAND-DADDY of service organization. The CCBA, and the merchants, they don't have anything! The only social service was only the Maryknoll Sisters and the Y, and they're both recreational, teeny...bit of adult education. There's nothing else!!

Its success in bringing the first social services to the community people provided useful information for strategies that other community agencies could use in establishing their goals, purposes and action plans. At the same time, community workers who first worked in the NCLEC diversified to various task forces to provide links and help for other community organizations that were eventually established.

In the agencies established a decade ago, community work, whether paid or non-paid, has attained a professional level. Community workers who got involved are educated individuals with some degree of professional expertise. The goal of these community organizations is to provide services, and the community worker tends to view the people as "clients"; they view the community as a "problematic area." Fainstein and Fainstein (1974:22,27) points out that community workers who work in these organizations are socializing agents on behalf of middle-class society offering opportunities for mobility to those able to take advantage of them. Moreover, their community work and activism reflect the middle-class value of assimilation, individual mobility and equal opportunity in terms of social opportunities through the provision of education and services, rather than a redistribution of income and power.

It is evident that many community workers come from a middle-class background, are mostly suburbanites and are university-educated and professionals. Thus, their decision-making reflects elitism of the system remaining in the hands of a few individuals and they have never involved community people in their decision-making. These various service organizations developed in Northville Chinatown as well as in other Chinese communities. In these particular agencies, unlike the old, traditional associations, the majority of these new community workers are educated and trained for the positions in the new organizations.

The Activist Stage

In the mid-1970's, an emergent group of community workers began to change the existing pattern of community work. In this study, I refer to them as "community activists," so as not to confuse them with the early 1970's group of community workers. These activists are active politically in advocating issues that concern third-world minority communities. The majority of them have lived at some point of their lives in the Chinese community as will be seen in the life-history that is given in the following chapter. They work closely with community people and are a group of zealous workers who realize the importance of community-based participation as well as the total lack of community power and control people have in their own community. When they move out of the community, they still identify with their original roots, i.e., the community and the Chinese-American experience. Formed partly by the activism they experienced in the early 1970's of the Asian-American Movement in college and the anti-Vietnam war movement of this country, their community participation remains important to them.

Involvement in the community means struggling for equality, working and organizing people for immediate issues that affect the community. These community activists are distributed in a number of organizations that developed in the mid-1970's. The key feature of these new agencies is the emphasis on grass-roots participation and around specific issues.

Three activist organizations are the Housing and Land Association, the Chinese Parent's Committee and the Tenants' Group Association. The Housing and Land Association primarily deals with problems and issues of encroachment. For example, when Ace moved in to acquire two buildings, most of the garment factories had to be relocated outside the community and some garment workers were laid off. The Chinese Parents' Committee deals with bi-lingual and busing issues, the Tenants' Group Association handles tenants' complaints, the cleaning and sanitation system, crime-watch, rent increases and legal procedures. The Chinese language is a key communication component here. The Housing and Land Association's meetings are held in Cantonese with English as a second language so as to include community people in the association and the meetings of all these associations are opened to members and all those who wish to join.

Grass-roots community organizations include the Chinese Progressive, Incorporated and the Chinese-American Experience Organization. These organizations are not funded by outside agencies. They obtain their resources from involved individuals and thus, they can advocate for the community without outside influence or pressure. Emily, an activist member of the Chinese Progressive, Incorporated, sees the importance of grass-roots organizations in Chinatown in the mid-1970's. She said:

> I think the progressive movement[7] has been moving forward and the formation of the Chinese Parents' Committee and the Tenants' Group in '75 marked the turning point for a lot of things in Chinatown. People see the need and want that kind of people's associations and organizations, which is a big change from the past when everything goes toward the established organizations ....The sentiment in the community now is that people are not afraid to speak up....and that people are able to do that on their own.

The community power lies in having decisions made by the people themselves and not in relying on the existing organizations, especially the ones that were established in the early 1970's, to solve their problems. As Jade, an activist lawyer said:

> The services didn't come about in Chinatown because the govern-
> ment feels that they could address everything we've got...I think
> for the 80's, it's important for people to fight for what we have,
> and to fight and maintain what we already have now.

The term "people" is used by activists to mean exclusively "people who live in the com munity." Activists stress that in order for an organization or group to function, it must include people in the community.

The grass-roots organizations that developed in the mid-1970's involved many com-munity people. For instance, the busing issue that affected the community in the mid-1970's. Emily emphasized the importance of people's involvement in the community. She said:

> Through my own experience with the parents and the women, when
> people see that unless they can do something, things then can
> change....like they formed the Chinese Parents' Committee, they
> boycott the school for two days to get what they wanted. For
> the School Department to address the safety issue, for them to
> hire Chinese-speaking people in the school so that Chinese pa-
> rents can have communications with the school...they do it!!
> They don't see what's the big deal.

She continued:

> I have to remind people that that was a very, a very important
> thing that they did to show that they have come together that
> we can...slowly change things, and that we can learn in the
> process.

In the mid-1970's and the late 1970's, the participation of Chinese people began to be more visible. A demonstration was organized in 1979 to fight against Ace University's encroachment in the community. In 1975, a demonstration was organized by the Chinese Parents' Committee on the school-safety issue. The parents boycotted the school for two days before measures were taken to ensure the safety of their children being bused out to the nearby school in Northville. This visible activism by Chinese people is a major step that grass-roots participation and organizing have produced. According to activists, the important result was not whether things changed overnight but that

38

Chinese people learned that as tenants or parents they are not the passive recipients

of services, but they have to go out and get whatever they want for their community.

San-san, a teacher activist for ten years said:

> It was really hard to get parents that involved because they
> come to this country feeling that education offered by this
> country is going to help their kids and they don't feel that
> they're here to criticize. Compared to the situation where they
> were coming from in Hong Kong or China, it was very little or
> nothing. I mean unless you have the funds to go to a private
> school in Hong Kong, or you go to the public school, and it's not
> that terrific. And then, they came here and they hear about the
> great schools and universities and also in general, Chinese
> have a high respect for the teaching profession that they don't
> feel that they're in a position to criticize what teachers do....

The same thing for involving people in holding up signs and marching in the

streets. A woman activist who organized people to do that was much admired by other

activists. San-san who saw what happened in the rally said:

> I got to hand it to her, I admire her for her willingness to
> take time away from her family. I think she has been able to
> tap more parents and Chinese-speaking people to get involved
> with issues like getting people, even elderly people to hold
> up the signs and marched [laugh a little], it's not that easy
> you know, she did it!!

Grass-roots activists are recreational as well. For instance, the Chinese Pro-

gressive, Inc. holds ping-pong tournaments, organize trips to places, and show films

from China. These are activities that are opened to all people. The organization

also opens on weekends and Friday nights so that workers who work late hours have a

place to meet and talk. Classes are held in Cantonese and Mandarin as well as in Eng-

lish so that Chinese-Americans can have a place to meet with the Chinese-speaking

people in Chinatown.

The activists that I met address not only specific issues but also larger issues

like socialism, the minority's position in society, women's position and Marxist Fem-

inist concepts. These women activists sensitized me to many important issues. One

time I blundered by referring to the passivity of the Chinese people and their re-

served character. Candice, an activist, challenged that:

I believed it's a myth. The common belief that Chinese people
are passive and then a lot of Chinese-American history is not
known to many people...As I dug through some of the history,
I was impressed with the kinds of struggle that has [sic] gone
on for the last 150 years that was waged by workers to address
the things that we're talking about to have some control over
their lives.
Starting with the railroad workers, there were strikes to win
equal pay. In Northville, there were attempts to organize
unions in restaurants way back in the 1930's...big struggle.
In the mid-1950's, too, there were a lot of open sentiment
in support of China, People's Republic of China, a lot of people was arrested. I don't think that we Chinese people are
passive, I think we need to dig into that kind of past history
and write a lot more about it.

The belief that Chinese people have the strength and the ability to fight and

struggle for their own community underlies the efforts to organize. Activists do not

quit easily because of their strong belief that the history of the Chinese-American

experience provides the possibility that there is a hope of a future for the Chinese

people and for changes to come about in the lives of the Chinese people in the commu-

nity.

Unifying different segments of the Chinese population to fight for their own rights

is the prime concern for all activists. Di, who spent most of her time in the Chinese

Progressive, Inc. Center, told me of her particular view:

My goal is to have equality for Chinese people, I think that
is the main concern [pause for awhile]...the main thrust of
this organization and my own personal feeling, but that what
is it that [is] going to unite the different sectors of Chinese people and how will Chinese people really win equality,
those are the main questions that people are facing right now.
Everyone has a different perspective.

Not only is that a different perspective in the strategy to unite the different

Chinese groups, but other activists like Emily feels that the organization should have

an overall concern for fighting for equality for Asian-American segments. Emily said:

The growth of the membership in the Chinese Progressive, Inc.
in the past year has come from the Asian-American sector,
which means that...we see that Asian-Americans have a general
interest in Chinatown.

This particular segment of Asian-Americans is still very small, and a few (three)

that I have come to know are half-Chinese individuals who feel that they identify more

with their Chinese roots. However, the strategy of uniting different segments of peo-

ple is the crucial point of discussion. Emily said:

> The question is: How do you get people involved, and encourage
> people to come back into the community...because I think the
> language question is a major factor, for most Asian-Americans.
> It's not their fault. Sometimes, it's very difficult for Asian-
> Americans to feel that they're wanted in their own community.
> We want to promote the view that American-born and the foreign-
> born [Asians] can work together. They're part of the whole
> sector.

Then, there is the question of whether to include the women as well as men into

more grass-roots participation. She said:

> Why women are more vocal, seem to me that they're more radical or
> progressive. A lot of them are Chinese-speaking and parents and
> tenants here are mostly women. I think that the reason is a lot of
> women in this society is oppressed here, particularly Asian women,
> that women are a lot more sensitive, to rebel against it.
> For Chinese-speaking women, well...they have to pick up a lot of
> organizing skills on their own, because of the time factor. You
> see most of the men have to work 'lot more hours and because of
> that, women are doing a lot more...also the men, the people they
> come in contact with are pretty much within the Chinese community
> that sometimes, they're not so aware or in tune with what's
> happening in our society at large than women are because...they
> have a lot more time than men, they're working, they're aware of
> the labor problems in the white society, their bosses are white...

Women not only have to take care of their children, but also face certain problems

in the workplace, for example losing their jobs because Ace University bought over the

area. These things have prompted women to make time, even though they have little

time for themselves, to go out and fight for their jobs. At some point, when educa-

tional issues come up, they must participate since their children are affected.

The activists that I interviewed address not only specific issues but also ques-

tions like feminism, socialism, the Chinese-American experience and history, minority

issues like racism, exploitation, and equality. This is unlike the social service

community workers who provide the conventional services described previously.

In looking at the three stages of development of community organizations and community work, we can understand better the importance of organizing the community to serve the different needs and interests of the different community sectors. Over the past ten years, growth of community work in Northville Chinatown has flourished. Community workers that I encountered realize the community work they do is essential. Their skills and strategy have matured as they learn through experience encountered in their work. However, community workers do not work alone. They see that they all together contribute to the community organizations, to the community itself and to the history of the Chinese-American struggle. Community work will continue and their devotion will keep them going, because they say, it is "for all of us."

CHAPTER III   GETTING INVOLVED: THE LIVES AND WORK OF COMMUNITY WORKERS

Not all women can become community workers. The continuous crisis management,
long hours, and high performance standards carry extreme pressure for women who work
in the community. Those who are involved see clearly that involvement affects their
personal lives and lifestyles. The women understand that involvement is not easy and
that they must set goals and priorities in what they can offer and contribute to the
community. More importantly, these women community workers emphasized that community
work requires a full personal commitment. The continuous flow of energy and immersion
on the part of the community workers is crucial to their job. Through shared goals
and values, the women make community work an important and necessary tool in serving
the needs of and maintaining the survival of the entire community. Thus, the community workers come together in Northville Chinatown in a collective action directed toward sustaining the life of the community.

Commitment refers to the obligations and willingness on the part of the individuals
to do what is best to maintain the group and the community organizations. It is based
in part on their desire for strong inter-personal relation with a collectivity, for
intense, emotional feeling among all members for sisterhood (brotherhood), and sharing.
This kind of relating contributes to the group cohesion that enables the community to
withstand threats to its existence, in the form of external pressure and tension and
dissent from within (Kanter, 1977:579).

Although there are different degrees of commitment, women community workers expressed that it was crucial to not only give and commit one's time and effort but also
to maintain their commitment. Ying, a board member of the Chinatown Community School,
pointed out that commitment must be encouraged and maintained:

> It is important to maintain a sense of consistency and a sense
> of energy and motivation, especially when you feel responsible
> for, and you're in a position to do that....

Each community worker has the responsibility to give support to others, and by her example, motivate others to be responsible. Emily, a teacher with whom I spoke, said that she, herself, has to take the lead when organizing the parents:

> It takes a lot of hard work in organizing. You have to show what you stand on, you have to be responsible for what you preach or what you say...and you say that people should fight for this and you're not there when the ship comes in, then FORGET IT [emphasis] ...[pause] you have to show that no matter what happens, you are there and that you don't disappear when things get difficult.

Being an activist herself, she showed that she is reliable and can be depended on to get things done. Through years of hard work, this teacher has come to play an important part in pushing for educational issues in the public school and for bi-lingual Chinese programs for the community.

Commitment is part of a learning process for women who are involved with community work. Some women, including me, when first starting to get involved do not realize the extent of commitment needed and how difficult it is to maintain it. It is not a learning process that happens overnight. For those who have stayed on for numerous years in the community, there is a high degree of commitment. Community workers themselves admire colleagues who stay on to work in the community, because no matter what kind of tasks they perform, it entails tremendous commitments of time and energy and does not come easy.

Rosabeth Kanter points out that the first step toward involvement entails the potential community work assessing the organization's goals and methods as similar to her or his personal orientation and preferences. She (1977:574) said:

> A person is committed to a relationship or to a group to the extent that he sees it is as expressing or fulfilling some fundamental part of himself; he is committed to the degree he perceives no con-flict between its requirements and his own needs; he is committed to the degree that he can no longer meet his needs elsewhere.... To a great extent, therefore, commitment is not only important for the survival of a community, but also is part of the essence of a community.

Community workers must consider the varying degree of their emotional involvement in the group and find ways to work for the community. Thus, the type of community work depends very much on the degree of commitment one gives to the community

In my study, I focus on four types of community workers who have selected the type of community work and the degree of involvement they want and are able to do. I called the four types of community workers: volunteers, professionals, officials and activists. Each type reflects differences in the relationships community workers have with the community and their approach to community work. In this chapter, I introduce two community workers in each category of volunteers, officials, professionals, and activists. The life-history here provides us with the reasons why they got involved and how each type gets involved with the community, so as to see the various social forces that influence their lives and their chosen work. Such factors as education, class background, family and children, outside professional work, and ideologies and principles, all play a major part in their becoming a committed worker. The latter part of this chapter focuses on the importance of subtypes and a brief discussion of the commitment each type of community workers has in her devotion to community work.

Volunteers

First, there are women who see themselves as volunteering their time to do community work. These women deal with the community on a small scale because their time is limited. They see community work as a secondary concern and they devote themselves to a number of small issues, or projects whenever they can. The volunteer work they do in various settings remains completely separate from their personal lives. They get involved "to do something," but that "something" is not well-defined, in terms of what they themselves can contribute. For them, community work is something to do when an opportunity arises. At some point, when another opportunity comes into their lives, they move on to another stage of their lives. They remain in a separate category from a professional or official because their commitment is never strong

45

enough for them to become more involved. Moreover, their involvement is not continous and of paramount concern because their own personal lives remain most important. Of the eight volunteers interviewed, five women are married; four have small children. Three out of the eight are singles in their twenties, two are in college, and one is leaving Northville for graduate school.

Community involvement remains secondary because they give precedent to their personal lives over the work they do in the community. Volunteers devote a minimum of two to five hours a week, but less hours when personal commitments conflict. For married women, family and children come first. When they can maintain the household, then they devote their time to doing community work in various capacities. For the single women, school work remains the primary concern. When finals and deadlines of papers approached, they spend less time doing work in the community.

The following section introduces two volunteer women community workers who are working in two different settings or organizations in the Chinese community. One is a housewife who lives in a northern suburb and the other is a graduate student who is completing law school in the area. In talking to these women, we can see that community work, though small scale, is important to them, and the experiences they have in doing community work develop their sense of doing something important for the community.

Ann: Editing Staff of the Community Newspaper

Ann is in her mid-thirties. She is tall and well-built. Her hair is fixed in a bun, tightly held back behind her head. When I first met her, her glasses and the way she talked reminded me of my Chinese school teacher I had when I was young. Ann speaks Mandarin and Cantonese fluently and as my interview with her progressed, our conversation switched among Cantonese, English and Mandarin.

Ann has four children. The youngest child is a toddler and Ann has to take care

of him at home. Ann came to this country as a student from Taiwan. As a college
student, she became involved teaching adult students in the community. After she got
married, she did not have anymore time. It was not until Ann met a woman community
worker that her interest in doing community work became renewed. The following is an
account of her involvement after college:

> I graduated in 1972 and I got married. My husband and I left
> the country for awhile and when I came back later on, I had my
> first child. A year later, that was in 1975, I was involved as
> a council board member of the Chinatown Community School. The
> involvement there was prompted by a senior person from the Chinese
> Community Church. She was around 68 years old...she passed away
> last year [1981], and was a very respected person in the community.
> Miss Cee was devoted to social services in Chinatown at an early
> stage before the professionals came in. She managed many, many
> immigration cases on her own and advocating for housing and jobs.
> She...[pause] took me and said: 'You come along, this is good for
> you.' At that time, I just wanted to see what's going on but she
> did initiate my involvement with the community school. However,
> that involvement wasn't too long, about a year or so, my second
> child came....

It was not until three years later that Ann became involved again. This time,
educational issues became important as her first child was enrolled in school. In
addition, her very close friend Sue, whom I interviewed also, got together with her
because Sue's children were in school. They became activist parents, advocating issues that are important in the public school system. She continued her account:

> Sue and I were both concerned about school. We started looking
> at some of the school issues, educational issues and some of
> the basics....The issue is that the Chinese community always
> react, react when the crisis comes down on us. I view that as
> a problem that Chinese community has to overcome before they can
> stand on their own feet. They have to stop being reactionary,
> but rather to anticipate...some of the things to happen. The
> first project that I was involved in was the bi-lingual imple-
> mentation plan. It is composed of teachers, parents, community
> leaders from all bi-lingual centers. We came up with the L-Plan
> before that, the city of Northville has no way to follow any
> plans and they can do whatever they want to do.

I then asked her about the L-Plan and what it does to the bi-lingual education
that the city has for minority students in the public school. She said:

47

There's a job description written for each level of personnel.
There are steps to be followed in how to identify a child as
a bi-lingual student; how to mainstream the child into the
regular program, which is a three-year period.

Before that, Ann believes that Chinese parents were not sophisticated enough to

assert their rights and concerns and the school system lacked experience in dealing

with bi-lingual children. She said:

At that time, we were coming from the parents' point of view,
that never dealt with [educational issues] before. Usually,
the bi-lingual parents are shy and busy; they don't speak
English. It's very difficult for other parents to go through
the process. Both Sue and I were not working so it put us
in a very unique position. Even though we tried only contacting a dozen parents...we were able to put together a very objective kind of representation in terms of the Chinese community.

That happened three years ago. Ann is still involved with the Parents' Council

that was created from that moment when parents got together to assert their right as

a group to have some say in the public school program. Today, she said that she is

still involved:

My present project is still continuing on what I'm doing. I'm
still in charge at the council. I see myself as a supporter;
let them make the decisions, I just am standing by to provide
technical assistance like writing letters.

Ann's involvement with the community has not lessened. She has become a volun-

teer journalist and editor for the Chinese section of the community newspaper, Dragon

Boat. She said:

I wrote a couple of articles before in the Chinese section and
then...someone called me up and asked whether I'm willing to
help out and I said, 'Well, it's probably a stage to really
start doing something more direct in the community.'

There are several reasons why Ann became active with the newspaper. One reason is

that her involvement with parents' educational issues in the school system affected

Northville Chinatown, but was also connected with the entire city. By changing cer-

tain things in the large public school system, she hoped that it would help the pa-

rents and school children in the minority communities in Northville. But she believed

48

it was time that she moved on to more direct involvement in the community. The news-

paper provides this opportunity to be involved. She explained:

> I see the immigrants' honeymoon years are over. They have to get
> into nitty-gritty things, they have to be able to stand on their
> own, that means another adult education. It has never been a
> classroom education, you never get them into a classroom. You have
> to orient them in various ways and media is one of the way to do it.
> Another reason I work for Dragon Boat is...my concern over the struc-
> ture of the Chinese family in Northville. The thing is that educa-
> tion is a good starting point to bring the family together. It's
> so much burden I have for Chinatown, even though people asked me,
> 'How can you do so much?' 'You're fine, you can quit now.' Well,
> I said, 'I haven't seen anything happening constructively among the
> family units. The parents, the school...' so as far as I can see,
> the newspaper is an instrument to bring more knowledge to issues
> that concerned family and children and school for these people.

Ann talked about things happening constructively. She wants to see results of im-

provements in the family. She feels the Chinese family remains in a difficult situa-

tion because the parents have to work and the children are left alone a great deal to

fend for themselves. In addition, there is a gap between the parents and the chil-

dren, exacerbated by the fact that there is so little time when the parents do not

work that they and the children can interact. Ann feels that this type of environment

is detrimental to the family as a whole.

Media are an important tool that one can use to educate. For three community work-

ers whom I came to know, including Ann, the newspaper is an important source of knowl-

edge for community people. Since 1980, Ann has made many improvements on the Chinese

section of the newspaper. The section is no long in hand-written print, and the type-

setting is cleaner so that one can read the articles more comfortably. More articles

and short items are translated from the English section on educational, job and family

issues; these are all content changes that Ann has worked for. The paper no longer

only covers diurnal events, but has expanded to a deeper level of imparting useful

knowledge to better enable community people and Chinese readers to make decisions

about the issues that concern their lives.

Ann feels that involvement with the newspaper means a personal growth as well. She said:

> My writing style has somewhat improved and changed. Oh yes,
> I forgot to say that another reason I got into Dragon Boat
> was to retain my Chinese.

She said that she will continue to work for the newspaper. To her, the community work that she has done and continues to do is valuable. She said:

> I feel that I'm one of the contributing members to society.
> By dealing with different parents, by dealing with different
> writers, and stories, I feel that I am contributing something.

Again, the word, "something" cannot be fully explained by the volunteer type of community workers because it encompasses a lot of different opportunities that she and others are opened to. Ann first got involved with the parents, then with the newspaper but she told me that she only works one or two days a week in putting all the materials together. In her career as a volunteer, there were a few "breaks" in her involvement because her family and children are important and she feels that she can only do so much. She said:

> Even though I'm with the parents' group and with Dragon
> Boat, my first obligation is to the kids. I still view
> that point as very important and that's why I don't go
> out that often. I view the family as a very strong unit.

Of the community workers who were married (five in the volunteer type of work), four who have children have a strong preference to place their families paramount in their lives. Community work to them is something that they do on the side, separate from their personal lives.

Ming: A Student Activist

Ming's time is very limited. I called her once and was asked to call back because she was very busy with law exams. A month later, I called and while I was making an appointment to come over to her apartment, she told me that there would be a

50

meeting with the garment workers to bring them to a relocation center outside the community. She asked me whether I could help and go with the garment workers because she had a seminar to attend. She was constantly busy. While being interviewed, she told me that I had only about one-and-a-half hours left because her friend was waiting in the library and they were going to study for an exam. She told me that her graduate work leaves her with very little time to do anything else, and only when she has time or makes time, would she get involved with the community.

Ming is twenty-four. She came to the United States when she was twelve years old. Her family lives in New York and after her graduation here she will return to New York and become a community lawyer. She speaks Spanish and English very well. When I first met her, I did not detect any foreign accent. It was only after she pronounced the word, "Caracas," that I detected her Spanish accent.

I find Ming a very mature person; partly because she is very clear on the issues that she is involved in and able to articulate her goals, her vision, and the problems in the community. She is such a serious speaker that sometimes it is difficult to believe that she is only twenty-four. Her experiences in community work has made her more mature than college students who do not work. For her, community work has inspired her career choice and she sees her law studies will be useful and related to serving the community.

I asked her how she first got started:

> I started long time ago, I did volunteer work when I was back
> in high school in New York City in the health clinic. I got
> involved with that from friends and sisters who were also in-
> volved in the community work. I was born in Caracas, Venezuela.
> My family immigrated to the United States when I was about
> twelve.

After she arrived in Northville for college, she did not get involved in anything because she did not know the community well enough. It was not until she joined the Eastern Asian Students Association that her friends introduced her to doing community work. She said:

51

> I met a lot of friends from the Eastern Asian Students Asso-
> ciation, and the Chinese-American Experience Organization is
> one place where a lot of my friends...we sort of founded the
> organization in 1979.
> A lot of my friends are musicians and artists and they want
> to teach that kind of stuff to the children in Chinatown.

Since Ming is in law school, she did her internship at the Northville Community Legal

Service Center and met another community worker (whom I came to know because of my

involvement with the health board in Chinatown). Ming said after she met Jade, she

began to work and volunteer in the Housing and Land Association in Chinatown. She

told me of her work in the association:

> I am involved [with the Housing and Land Association], but on
> and off. I use to work my first internship with Jade so when-
> ever she needs me to help her out, I do so. I go to law school
> and it's really hard for me to go a lot of times when Jade needs
> some research in a particular issue like zoning laws and stuff
> like that, I try to help her out in different ways in whatever
> I could. So she asked me why don't I come to the meetings and
> bring some ideas because when I talked to her, I would come up
> with ideas and she said that it would be good if other people
> in the Association hear about them.

Because of her school work, she said:

> I can't give an exact amount of time that I'm involved; it's
> like when you have to have a project ready, you do a lot of
> things around then and if you don't have a project then you
> don't do much. I used to do a whole lot more when I was in
> my undergraduate years, but law school is kind of tough and
> I spend more time in the library.

I asked her why then did she want to participate so much if she does not have

much time. She said:

> It keeps me in touch with a lot of people. I think it also
> makes me feel...[pause] a little bit different from being in
> school all the time and there is a lot of satisfaction when
> you do things.

She has learned a lot in doing community work. Self-improvement and self-develop-

ment are primary pay-offs in that community work gives volunteer workers a place

where one can grow. Ming told me:

> I used to be very, very shy--very shy. You would never catch
> me on a stage or anything like that. The more volunteer types
> of work you do, you discover there is no limit to what you can do.

Because there are a lot of opportunities, in fact, they're
crying out for people to volunteer because there are not
enough people to do things in the community

From this learning experience, Ming pointed out that community work, in fact, benefits

the individuals who are involved. She said:

It's better to learn to speak up because I think that's one
of the problems with a lot of Asian women who are quiet.
You're not so threatened and after you speak up for a couple
of times, you know you can do it, you can do it anywhere.

Community work on a volunteer basis allows community workers to move and grow apart

from their existing work experience. It will always remain that way. Community work

is a stage, a place in their lives, and like Ming, women volunteers in this community

will continue to move in and out. Because they define their lives as separate from

the work they do, they have no strong sentiments to stay. Ming told me that after

she finished school here, she will return to New York:

That's my hometown: my parents are there and I've been
offered a job so I guess I want to go back.

The Commitment of the Volunteers

The commitment of volunteers is not as great as professionals, officials and ac-

tivists. This is because the community work they perform is on a smaller scale. For

example, tasks that need to be done like bringing the displaced garment workers to

see the new office and factory sites, and visiting the refugee families. When one

volunteer cannot make it for work, she calls up and asks someone else to do it. Be-

cause they do not hold major positions in the organization, it is easier for volunteers

to turn down the tasks when they are busy with their family or schoolwork.

In the course of my interviews and fieldwork with eight volunteer community work-

ers, I found that four out of the eight will eventually leave this community. Three

students, including Ming, will be leaving once school is over. She already has set

plans to leave for New York, and two are going to California after the year (1982)

53

is over. One volunteer, who is married is uprooting her family because her husband has found a job in Asia.

Of the eight volunteer community workers interviewed, seven are not working outside in the labor force. Of the married women volunteers, four have children and live in the suburbs. Commuting to the city requires a great deal of effort and time. Three community workers who do volunteer work do not want major responsibilities because their families come first and managing the family is not easy for them. Ann told me that she was very grateful that the telephone makes her work with the community newspaper easier. Without the telephone, she would have a difficult time because she does not have a car and does not know how to drive. Thus, geographical distance and family responsibilities play a major part in the amount of work volunteers can do and the types of community work they have selected. More importantly, family and residential location affect their degree of involvement and commitment to community work.

For the single volunteer community workers, the community offers them opportunities to see themselves grow and improve their self-esteem and their identity. However, they cannot commit themselves to do more because their school or professional job outside the community makes them less flexible and is a transitional stage of their lives. They know that they will move on to other kinds of careers or opportunities when the time comes; therefore, taking on a major responsibility or position in the community is not easy for them. Volunteer community workers see that they have limitations on what they can do even when time and the opportunity arises, and choosing the right type of volunteer work is crucial so that when the time comes to leave, they do not feel a strong attachment to the community that would affect them. Thus, community work to these volunteers, whether married or single, is doing "something" useful and contributing "something" to the society. In time, the "something" that they have done adds meaning to their personal lives.

Professionals

The women professionals in my study are working full time in community organizations. They are fully qualified for the paid positions they hold in the various community organizations. Their work is well defined and because they work full time in the community, they are more visible than other community workers who spend less than five days or forty hours a week in the community.

All eight women I interviewed in this category had finished college. Five are from the social work and sociology backgrounds. However, not all the women I interviewed obtained their respective jobs in the agencies because of their educational qualifications. Three of the women had sat on the board of the community organizations and had a long history of active participation. Because of their record, they were recommended to be considered for the administrative jobs opened in the agencies. These women community workers have worked in the community for a long time and intend to stay on as long as they are needed. Four women in my study have stayed in their organizations for more than ten years; three have worked for more than five years. Only one had just started working a year ago.[1] These women community workers placed extreme importance on their jobs and they are committed to stay in the community. The loyalty to their community organizations and the community reduces the turnover rate for community professionals.

Community organizations are funded by external sources. The salaries are not very high. In a few cases, the positions are on a short-term basis. I have met women community workers taking one job after another after their funded contract ran out. With the recent cuts on the federal level, positions in the community organizations have been cut or frozen and when community positions are opened, most are funded on a short-term basis. A community worker who took a position in the after-school program funded by the city told me that she will not see her job two years from now. At this point,

55

she is looking for a more permanent position outside the community or she will go bac
to school to obtain more professional skills. Another woman community professional
whom I tried to include in my study refused to be interviewed. She told me over the
phone that in the past eight years, she had been working in one job after another unt
she became so frustrated about the funding uncertainty. She no longer works in the
community, and said that making her talk about her experiences in community work woul
upset her very much. For women community workers who stayed on their jobs, the low
pay and long hours are not that important because their personal priority is job sati
faction. Their primary concern for the community is to ensure that their organizatio
are providing good community services and reducing social problems for their respecti
clients who seek help. Most do not take long vacations away from their work, not because they love their jobs so much but because there is very limited help to take up
their workload in their absence. Since funding is scarce, administrators or social
workers must perform extra tasks that are normally done by their staff. This is a
reality that they have come to grips with. For long-time professionals, working in t
community is a way of life. It is a job and a challenge, and their performance is no
only evaluated by the staff and board but also by the community, who know these women
behind the agencies that care for them as concerned community workers.

Of the eight women I interviewed, four are married, three are single and one is
divorced. Among the eight women who are employed by various community organizations,
five held administrative positions and three held staff positions. Because the servi
agencies in the community are long established, their administrative or social work
positions are more secured than those that are funded by short-term contracts. Their
work involves writing grant proposals, budget plans and allocations, program development and implementation, hiring of social service employees and recruiting volunteers
maintaining relations with the board and seeking support and approval, contacting oth
community organizations (touching base) and maintaining links with outside agencies.

56

The following section introduces two community workers who are known professionals in their fields. One is an administrator in an adult education agency and the other is a social worker who does outreach work in the community concerning health issues. They have worked in the community for ten and eight years respectively and expect to stay. They see their jobs as important and would like to see the services expanded rather than eliminated. Their jobs are demanding especially because they are short of staff help and funding. However, they are determined to persevere through the hard times ahead.

Ling: An Administrator

Ling is the administrative coordinator of the Adult Education School in Northville Chinatown. She was formally a social worker with Ace University Hospital after she graduated from college; however, she later decided to work in administration. Through a friend she heard about the vacant position of this school and she applied. Since 1976, she has been the main administrator.

Ling is in her thirties. She is single and is a fourth generation Chinese-American brought up in Northville. She said, "I'm a native here; Northville is my hometown." And then she started laughing in a relaxed way. Her style of relating to people is carefree and easygoing. When I visited her office she told me that the interview would be interrupted occasionally because her secretary was away and she would have to act as director, secretary and receptionist at the same time. So I prepared myself for a long interview and came away quite surprised that I was able to finish her interview in about two hours, even though we were interrupted by a few clients coming in and several phone calls.

I first asked her how she got started working for the adult education center. Ling replied:

I'm not sure exactly how I got started [laugh]...I targeted
in a specific field...which is social work. At that time,
initially, it didn't matter whether or not I was in casework
or in a hospital or a private agency.

She eventually became a social worker after finishing college. She continued:

What happened was in my first job at the hospital [near the
Chinese community], part of my job involved cases that were
from the Chinese community--that's part of my responsibility.
Eventually that started the whole process, i.e., the community was growing. We needed more social services and we were
trying to deal with that. I was also involved with agencies
that just got started in the community...but more so with
clients.

That was ten years ago when she first began working with the Chinese recipients' ser-

vice and gradually she began to look for a job in the community.

I was looking for a job at that time. I wanted an administrative job. I thought I'll combine my direct service experience
with administration and planning. It just happened that one of
my colleagues on the board here was aware that I was available
and the director at the time took a leave of absence. They decided that she was not really coming back so the position came
to me.

Being an administrator, Ling is in charge of the overall operation of the center.

She does a lot of program development, budget planning and allocation, proposal and

grant writing, and hiring of the staff. However, she also maintains links with other

agencies in the area, on the outlook for possible opportunities to extend her agency's

programs and seek additional resources. She called this "touching base", and sees the

necessity of maintaining relations with outside community organizations as well as in-

side agencies. Her main concern is still the clients that come in to obtain help.

She said:

I like to see ideas develop and actually get implemented.
Get the services to the clients that we're aiming into
and seeing the clients succeed.

How does she know that the clients succeed?

We get feedback. Our clients come in here and they know a
certain amount of English. They know much more when they
leave here. They even know a lot more about survival skills,
job-hunting skills and career choices. Sometimes, they

58

complain that the more choices we give them, the...crazier
they'll get....[laugh]. But that's part of our job too.
Letting them know what they have to offer is valuable to
somebody; somebody is interested in them.
We have to see them to go into job placement or see them
go back to school. Often, they go into technical training
school or they go to four-year college.

Her schedule is busy. Even after work, she sometimes takes her work home with her.
er hours must be flexible; not nine to five. She sometimes has to visit other agen-
ies to find ideas and resources. Going outside of the community is necessary in order
o seek out potential resources. This is necessary not only to Ling but to other com-
unity workers I met. Ling told me:

There is always some help to us in terms of developing
additional funding resources. So sometimes I incorporate that in my work hours or my own hours to seek these
opportunities. It all depends upon what is convenient at
that particular time.

hese community workers also maintain links with places outside the city. Contacting
eople is an important part of the job and it is not rare to find a woman away from
er office and not expected back for several days because "she's out of town."

Because of the position Ling holds in the organization, going away for vacation,
specially long ones, is not possible. Ling told me:

Are you kidding? I haven't taken a vacation for about three
years. I talked to another friend about vacation. I don't
want to mention his name but you know, we haven't taken any
vacation for a long time. What...gets me is dealing with
things when you came back. It's worse that you have to trust
some people when you're gone and...you can't find yourself
when you come back.

In the environment that community workers deal in, a crisis arises sometimes with-
ut prior anticipation, as do the opportunities. Working full time in the community
emands that the community workers be on top of things when they happen to know the
hings that need to be done, and to be flexible enough to take on the sudden occur-
ences and problems in their work. Therefore, it is important to them that they are
resent to deal with it. It is common that worries of their jobs affect their person-
l life. The recent budget cuts and canceled grants mean that they must spend more

59

time in addition to their nine-to-five schedule to make things happen. Therefore, they have no set plans for leisure, especially long vacations away from their job. It is very difficult for Ling and other community workers to plan a summer vacation, rather, they take one or two days off at a time. This is the only strategy they have to combat fatigue from overwork.

Ling told me that community work is a learning process, and is not an easy job to do. The long hours, low pay, and short vacation breaks are job conditions that can only be withstood by a special group of workers. It is not money and promotions that attract community workers but the satisfaction of providing help and services and seeing tangible results. Reflecting on her working experiences, Ling said:

> I learn to make big commitment and stay with it. To combine
> what you have now with what you have already done to build on
> it. At this point, I love to get a job with any company and
> go to Europe....[laugh] I like to think that there are other
> openings for me in different types of organizations, but then
> ...I'm not sure, I like to stay....I love community work and
> I have made that commitment.

Most community workers make the choice to remain at their agencies. And for Ling who targeted her college education towards social services; her skills have paid off in a well-managed adult education center that is developing under her supervision. Seeing the clients succeed in getting a job, learning survival skills, and in being able to work in a good job is the sole satisfaction and reward she derives from her work in the Chinese community.

Angie: A Social Worker

Angie is a single woman in her late thirties. She came to the United States as a college student from Hong Kong. She completed her undergraduate degrees in socie logy and psychology, and then moved to social work for her graduate study. Angie was a social worker for eight years in a small town in New York state. She found life very lonely there and decided to move. Through a relative in Northville, she heard

bout a job opening in the Chinese community. In 1974, she became a social worker for
he health center in Chinatown and has been here for eight years. She said about her
ob:

> I like working with the people in this community. It's like
> serving my own people and I like it here. And I do not think
> that I will find another job anywhere else.

he speaks Cantonese fluently, and this makes her job easier since the majority of the
hinese population she serves speak Cantonese.

As a social worker she created the first outreach program in Chinatown. It be-
ame so successful that other organizations in the Chinese community modeled them-
elves on Angie's programs. She said:

> I do group work. This is part of social work, and is seldom
> used because most social workers [work] with single or indi-
> vidual cases. The difference between group work is that it
> requires more work on the part of the social worker to get a
> group together. It's more demanding and you have to have a
> good training experience to get this type of work together.

ngie decides the group programs at the health center. The programs promote health
are by involving children, adults and the elderly in the community. It is difficult
o start a group work program, Angie said, when:

> ...the health center is only one-year-old and in order to
> reach the people, I have to knock on doors and...the resi-
> dents know that the health center is doing something for
> them.

ventually, she widened her contacts to include not only women and children but also
amilies, and bring them as a unit into her program at the health center.

She works in the daytime, except during the summer months when the health center
rovides more recreational programs. Then she must work in the community on weekends,
ringing groups around the city or parks. She said, "In a way, I am promoting the
ental health of the people in the community." Her work schedule varies from forty
ours to sixty hours a week during the summer months. The week that I interviewed
er, she was involved with the Health Fair to be held in the community on that Sunday.

61

She was busily making contacts, not only to involve the residents but also people in different community organizations in the one-day event. I asked her whether networking is important. She said:

> It is very important. I have to know most of the people who
> are working in different agencies, but usually I know these
> people from working with them. As for my clients, I have to
> build trust...you have to make sure that people can rely on
> you...you have to show them that you are doing things that is
> valuable to them. It took me a long time to build my network
> and my programs....[pause and then spoke softly] not easy.

As the person in charge of the health center, she finds that the work is extremel taxing. In her department she finds herself overworked; she does not have professional assistance from the health center. Since I knew Angie before I interviewed her, I often found her at home during weeknights and I asked her why when we were having dinner together at her house one day. She said:

> My job is not easy. I come home very tired. It's like I
> want to retire early and prepare myself for another
> lo-o-o-ng day....

As for vacation, she has not taken one for almost two years, but would like to take one if there was a way for some colleagues to cover her job.

Like Ling, Angie is determined to stay at her job in the community. She told me that her satisfaction is derived from seeing her clients become independent and learning the survival technique for living in a different and new environment. Since most of her clients are new immigrants, she sees the change in them after they complete the program at the health center. This kind of improvement makes her feel good about working with people. She said:

> I still want to deal with the social aspect of social work,
> that's what I'm trained to do....one has to stay long [enough]
> in the community in order to see the results. Sometimes
> it is very frustrating if I only look for immediate effects,
> because when I work hard I like to see things happening.
> But...my main goal is to see an overall improvement in human
> relationships--nothing for myself.

asked her what she wants to see in the community as a social worker who has worked
ere for eight years. She said:

> Well, I like to see more people doing the same kind of work
> that I'm doing. Group work, you know, not individual cases.
> I think that's an important approach for people in the commu-
> nity, their overall well-being.

hen, she added:

> Oh, by the way, I'd like to see the health center bring in
> another assistant, I'm overworked!!

he last remark was aimed at me, as I am a member on the board of the health center.

owever, both Angie and I know that funding is being cut and it is not possible for

his to happen in the near future.

The Commitment of The Professionals

It is interesting to examine the work history of these professional women. I

ound that of the eight women interviewed, seven women started their first jobs as

rofessionals outside the community. It is only when they started getting in touch

ith community people or workers that told them about a position open in the community

rganizations, that they applied. Thus, identifying with "helping the Chinese people"

id not occur until after they worked in the community. It was then that they found

heir job in the community rewarding and it was expected that they would continue to

ork in the Chinese community.

Like the volunteers, professionals find that they are happy when they can see

their clients succeed or become independent. Moreover, professionals also treat their

involvement in the community separately from their private lives. Involvement means

doing a job that needs to be done, but unlike the volunteers, the job is a responsi-

bility they take seriously. However, it remains clear in their mind that their commu-

nity job is separate from their family or personal lives. When I asked professional

staff and worker whether they give their phone numbers to their clients in case of an

63

emergency, the general answer is "no." I asked what happens if the elderly or families need emergency help. They answered that they could go by themselves to the near-by hospitals or call their relatives. Very rarely are phone numbers given out. This separation of their private and public lives is essential, for the most common complaint or problem in a human service organization is that it is understaffed; many community workers are overworked. The demands are unending and they can only do so much. Thus, it is not surprising that the burn out syndrome among the staff and administrators in these agencies is high. This makes it even more important to maintain the boundaries between professional and private life.[2]

Community workers who have stayed long enough in the community see that the organizations have matured. There are more professionals in the community now than ten years ago, and these professional community workers have done a lot to keep the community organizations going for so many years. The year 1982 marks the tenth anniversary for most of the community organizations that provide social services in the community. It is time for the professionals to look back and rejoice in what they did in creating programs, in seeing their funding continued, and their clients succeed in the American society. The celebration is a tribute to these professional community workers who have the determination to stay and who made the big commitment to work for the community.

Officials

The board of directors in a community organization is a policy and decision-making unit. Women community workers who sit on the boards are officials who determine the goals and focus attention on specific areas and events in the internal departments of the organization. They also deal with budget planning and approval, fundraising decisions and projects as well as program action. The administrators in the organization constantly seek board support and approval for the implementation of their plans.

64

Most community workers who have an interest in health or education try to obtain membership for their respective organizations or other agency boards in the community that are related to their interests. These board members are professionals working full time outside their community interest areas. The annual board meeting held by every organization is a time when new and old community workers exchange views of positions and renew their interests. There is a large number of medical professionals as well as medical administrators from various nearby hospitals on the health board. On the school council, a few are in the teaching profession and others are educational administrators. However, not all community workers need such backgrounds to join the board; there are others who are just interested in joining. For me, it was my friends' urging that led to my interest, and I know a number of other new members were brought in because of their friends' persuasions.

The boards in the community organizations consist of old and young individuals. The older generation of officials are people who first got involved with community organizations in the earlier part of the 1970's. They called themselves, the "old vanguards." In my study I interviewed two vanguards who were founders of a number of organizations. Vanguards have enriching experiences in organizational management in Northville Chinatown because they have been in these agencies longer than other community workers. When I first came into the community organizations and told my community worker friends about getting involved, they called me "young blood"; not because I was younger than them, but because I was new to community organizations and did not go through community politics as much as they had done when organizations first got started. The younger generation of community workers that came after the mid-1970's are called the "young bloods." The old vanguards welcome the sight of younger generations of Chinese-Americans coming to work in the community and providing new ideas and ways of dealing with problems. In most cases, the combination of older and younger generations on the boards provides interesting perspectives and group dynamics.

65

These officials are not full-time workers in the community; and the board, committee, subcommittee and ad hoc committee meetings are all held on weeknights and week ends for the convenience of those who work for their living. The schedule of the meetings is varied. The health board meeting is held on the second Tuesday of every month whereas the school board meeting is held on the first Tuesday of every month. However, each organization's subcommittees held weekly meetings if necessary to get things done. For example, the banquet committee meets once every two weeks, but when the banquet date was drawing near for their tenth anniversary celebration, the group met at least once every week to solicit funds, get the programs printed, and other necessary activities. The personnel committee that I am involved with at the school holds meetings depending on the necessary reports and interviews to be done for the administrators' annual evaluation. During the summer we met regularly once a week.

Officials' schedules are very tight. I have met some community workers that sit on the boards of three different organizations and their personal lives evolve around other community workers. Although community workers are able to separate their work lives and community involvement, the separation between community involvement and personal lives for officials is not so clear-cut as compared to the volunteers. Their ideology, vision, and goals of their personal lives play an influential part in their commitment to community development. Whereas the volunteers spend time to help whenever they can; their convictions are not as strong and their priorities are not as community-related as those of the officials.

In the following section I introduce two different officials, each of whom sat or is sitting on the board of two different organizations in Chinatown. Both have overlapping memberships in other community organizations and have assumed leadership roles (both are or were chairpersons) on their respective boards and are well respected. Jean is an old vanguard who came to Northville before the mid-1970's and is influenced by the 1960's social movement. In contrast, Jade came in 1978 and is considered a

66

"young blood" in community work. Her community experience was derived from her in-

volvement in the establishment of New York's Chinatown health center. She brings a

different perspective in advocating for community issues. Together, Jean's and Jade's

interesting backgrounds provide us a view of the older and younger generation of commu-

nity workers who are officials in the community organizations.

Jean: An Old Vanguard

Jean is a professional woman I interviewed two years ago while doing my study on

Chinese women and their professional careers. At that time, Jean was a research fellow

at a university in Northville. She earned a doctorate degree in education and wanted

to open a consulting company in developing educational and training programs for insti-

tutions. Two years later, Jean's dream came true. She has her own consulting company

and her hard work has paid off.

She is in her late thirties, still single, and active in the community. She trav-

els quite often for business engagements, and on her way to the West Coast, would stop

by to see her family. Jean is a third-generation Chinese-American and grew up on the

West Coast. In 1974, she came to Northville for graduate studies and began her commu-

nity involvement here. Jean was brought up to be involved in community work from an

early age. She said the 1960's movement influenced her outlook and her self-motiva-

tion, and she will continue her active participation on the community level. She said:

> My sense is that my comfort level and my ability to operate
> in the black and Chinese communities is really...[pause] from
> a young age. I was able to deal with that. Community involve-
> ment was a growing sensitivity of the 1960's. I got involved
> with the Civil Rights Movement....

When that was over, she continued to be very active.

As I was listening to her life story, Jean truly surprised me, for I interviewed

her in 1979, and yet her life story was never revealed in such detail. She became a

Civil Rights participant in the 1960's and traveled down South. Later, she traveled

67

to Thailand with a missionary, then came back to the United States and worked for a

number of years in Harlem and Chinatown in New York City. For about forty-five minute

of our conversation, she recounted her interesting life before she reached Northville.

Community work to Jean is important and she would continue her involvement no matter

where she goes:

> Many years ago, a priest gave me a nickel. I need to borrow a
> nickel for parking or something. He's a friend of mine and I
> tried to give the nickel back and he said, "No, don't give it
> back to me, I'm glad to give it to you, I had it." So he said,
> "The next time somebody asks you, you give her or him a nickel."
> And I always look for someone to give a nickel because I felt
> so guilty that I couldn't give back what I've taken. I think
> that's my attitude. My attitude is that somebody gives me some-
> thing, so I might...give it to others. My main attitude is
> that community work is not separate to my way of thinking, it's
> just my life, I will always serve the community, because it's
> just payment of what is given to me.

When Jean came to Northville, she missed doing community work. So she tried to

enter the community. This opportunity arose when she met a local politician. She

related:

> I met Mr. K [a black community leader in Northville] through
> friends and he suggested that I should hook up with Ben Lee
> [director of the Chinatown Economic Affairs Organization].
> So...then I served on the board where I still serve.

Jean not only is active on the board but also in other communities. She said:

> I'm on the board of Searle Community College and also on the
> board of Minority Job Workshop; mainly because of my profes-
> sional interests in education and manpower.

In getting on these boards, she said:

> A black woman friend of mine knew that I was really interested
> [in] education, and knew that I was in the university's educa-
> tion department and she also knew that I'm running a company
> and thought that it would be good for me to be on the board.
> I'm also on some national boards, no, national committees.
> I always will be interested in community work.

Jean has continued to serve on these boards for years and her goal in life is to not

separate her professional interest and her personal life. She said:

68

One is that I want everyone to be able to have a chance
to be educated and have a job....since I know the game
and how to do it,...and since I know at what level I can
convey that, meaning serving on the boards, giving people
access to information and knowledge, then I might do it.
What I do with my professional life, I just carry over
to my personal life. To me, there's no difference between
personal and professional

Jean's schedule is very tight. She not only runs her consulting company but also

works weeknights with members of different boards and committees in developing

projects. At the same time, she takes care of her adopted son who is in elementary

school. She said:

Ben Lee [the director of Chinatown Economic Affairs] demands a lot of my time....like this week, he came in to
spend an hour with me at the office. I called Shin [some-
one else who is on the board] yesterday. I'll be having
breakfast with him tomorrow, and probably with him Friday.
So I would say I give easily ten or twenty hours a week,
easily...hmm, just for community activities.

Jean's current project on the board is manpower and education. She explained:

We're trying to create a...training corporation in Chinatown. Because there's no training money, we want to figure
out how to train people and make money out of it. The reason we wanted to be profit-making is because it must be self-
sustaining so it doesn't have to rely on federal funds.

This is not only Jean's philosophy, but also that of many community workers who are

looking at other resources. Since the past few years, community workers have been

looking at various places to seek funding, since federal funding is running out in a

lot of community organizations. Time spent on the search for other directions and

alternatives is crucial and is the responsibility of many board officials.

To Jean and other women community workers, going to board meetings is a learning

process. Jean said:

I REALLY [emphasis] learn how to deal with business matters;
how to deal with human relations level and how to deal with
financial level. I just sit there and listen, but I listen
to the group dynamics. I learn more in board meetings than
anywhere else.

In addition, women community workers learn how to phrase their thoughts and how to handle different issues. Women learn to accept responsibilities and deal with them professionally. At meetings, community workers learn to accept challenges and deal with decisions and policies that other areas of work do not provide. In community work this particular level of participation is fruitful in that it provides a training ground and a stage for community workers to perform their part as officials.

Jade: A New Blood

Jade is a community lawyer and has worked in Northville for the past four years. What is unusual about Jade is that she has a wider interest of participation in advocating for community issues, such as unionization, housing and health care. In addition to her participation on the health board in Chinatown, she is a lawyer representative of the Land and Housing Association. In the latter association, she strongly advocates for grass-roots participation, even though she is not a grass-roots organizer. She hopes that in the future the health center, as well as other social service agencies, will have greater participation by community people on the board level.

Jade is in her early thirties and is single. When I interviewed her at her office, the first thing that she talked about is her community involvement in New York. She started talking about her family background:

> I'm originally from New York. I grew up in New York's
> Chinatown and my family first immigrated to this country
> in 1959. So I spent the last...I guess, twenty years
> in Chinatown and then four years in Northville.

Community involvement for Jade started when she was in high school tutoring to Chinatown children. Later, she became involved in health care issues in New York's Chinese community. With the experience gained in organizing a health fair event in New York, she and a group of friends began to plan creating a neighborhood health center. The health center is successful, but when it first opened in a church, most

70

of her time was spent in making the center survive. During this phase of community

work, she began to realize that obtaining better skills is important in working in the

community. With that in mind, she said:

> I went to law school, thinking that going to law school
> would help develop better skill to work in the community.
> After I got out of law school, I decided that I want to
> work at the legal service office, mainly because I was
> interested in becoming a community lawyer...that kind of
> practice can help the low income and third world people.

Four years ago, she moved to Northville to continue her career goal, that is to be a

community lawyer dealing with civil cases. In Northville, she was interested in

health care and decided to join the health board here.

Jade told me that she did not have any friends on the health board when she first

came to Northville and so,

> I initiated the contact by sending a letter to the health
> center's board and say I'm interested and...here's my back-
> bround. Lum [the president on the health board] contacted
> me and I joined the board.

Her main motivation and ideology are interwined. For the officials who are the "new

bloods," getting involved in the community stems from their own beliefs and ideologies.

Jade is a model. The ideology is part of an official's personal life and what she

wants to do for herself and for the community. Jade describes this:

> I think there are different kinds of motivations. The most
> basic one is my belief that...the Asian community has got
> to get organized in order to create social change. But I
> think for me, it's something that I hope will stay with me
> for the rest of my life in believing that...it is possible
> to create social change and it is possible for the community
> to do that kind of organizing. That's the big piece of it.

Community workers who are officials do not get on a board in a community organi-

zation just to do "something." They are different from the volunteers. For the new

bloods and the old vanguards, the board has the power to change things, to organize

and realize policies for the present and the future. Before joining the board, the

community workers already have a clear perspective of what they want the organizations to do. And, through their input, the community workers hope to achieve personal

satisfaction in making things happen   in the community.

Jade participates not only on the board of the health center. Like Jean, she is

also very active in other community organizations. Jade has been involved with the

Housing and Land Association for four years. She told me that she is very keen and

interested in that organization, mainly because her expertise is needed. She said:

> Someone from the association called me and said that they were
> looking for a lawyer on an issue that they were working on.
> I went for a couple of meetings and got interested in some of
> the issues they were working on, and have been involved ever
> since.

In legal matters, especially in the areas of housing and tenants, she took time

out to do research and represent the association at various hearings. Eventually her

outspokeness on these issues gained public attention in Northville.

Her schedule is packed with meetings. When she assumed the responsibility of re-

presenting the tenants, she took on more work than she can handle. However, communi-

ty workers are used to a lot of meetings. Like Jean, she checked her calendar in fron

of her and told me offhandedly:

> This week...well, there's a board meeting tomorrow; there's
> a fundraising meeting on Wednesday. I have the Land and
> Housing Association's meeting on Friday...[pause] Oh, I
> also have another housing meeting tonight.

These meetings sometimes leave community workers exhausted. Community workers who had

full-time jobs have a long, hard day and still have meetings at night. It is not un-

usual to hear grumbling during the meeting, and wishes are put forward that the meet-

ing will not be a long one. However, when the matters at hand are important, the meet

ing can drag on to very late hours. Usually, community workers return home sometimes

around ten o'clock and then they prepare to retire and to face another long day at

work. This kind of lifestyle is not easy. For those who have a family and children

at home, arrangements must be made. Not all community workers can withstand these

long days. Sometimes, officials find it difficult to commit themselves to this kind o schedule. Attendance is low, especially just before the year's term of membership is ending. Attending these meetings requires extra effort and energy on the part of the officials.

Officials like Jade who stay on for so many years give community involvement high priority. Their personal and social lives must conform to suit their busy work schedule. Unlike the volunteer who place their family and children, or their studies and career paramount, officials placed community work side by side with their career as their main goal in life. This is possible for nearly all officials when their general interest in the full-time jobs they hold, whether in the community or outside, coincides with their interest in community issues and problems. For example, Jean's interest in manpower and development coincides with the community organization. Jean's career as a lawyer deals with community issues, and outside the working schedule, she also deals with community issues.

Active officials with a long-term involvement like Jade form only a small minority group. Jade states her own commitment very clearly by using the comparison of professional community workers and officials like herself as a reference point to the priority of community work to community workers like herself:

> They [the professionals] are very good in doing community jobs,
> but they also see that community jobs were separate from parts
> of their lives. They basically go to work, from nine to five
> or whatever, and they have a very separate life outside the com-
> munity. I don't mean to suggest that's a bad thing to have,
> I think you need people to be performing a direct service func-
> tion...BUT [emphasis] you need people to be consistent and be
> in the community for a long time and not burn-out....

Commitment is important for those who work in the community. This entails consistently being involved or else community work will not be accomplished. However, not many community workers do that. Jade told me there is a way:

> The way to do it is to have some separation between their role
> of professional lives and personal lives. But then there are
> people like myself who grew up in Chinatown and feel strongly
> about issues and made less of a separation between their profes-
> sional lives and their personal lives.

73

This is an important point. The "new bloods" in the community are beginning to learn about prioritizing their lives.

When asked about her future direction and what she would like to see in the community organizations that are service-oriented, she replied that she would like to see more grass-roots participation on the community organizations' boards. This idea has not worked so far because of the language barrier, as the meetings are conducted in English. She told me such organizing to change the community is still a vision:

> I'll love to get a community board that will compose of fifteen percent patients. consumers and have meetings in Chinese. That's a very long-term goal, the community is not at that place yet. We tried to do it with the board last year. We had some non-English speaking patient representatives on the board. It didn't work out very well. They were not interested in the issues that we were talking about.

As long as Jade and many "new bloods" continue to be committed, community development will change in the future.

The Commitment of The Officials

Though many officials move in and out of the community organizations, the active officials who remain in the organization for a long period of time are important backbones to these organizations. In addition, many community workers (officials) are on different boards of organizations in the Chinese community. I have met some community workers who sit on the boards of three different organizations and are completely immersed in these meetings, projects and events in addition to holding a full-time job. For me, my two board involvements leave me very little time to socialize outside the community organizations' meetings, especially when immediate projects become necessary. Overlapping board memberships, like Jade and Jean do provide useful linkage and representation either with the community or outside the community that are sometimes useful. The two community organizations in which I am involved have planned

74

joint events and joint board meetings that proved to be very successful. In time, such linkage provides unity, co-operation and strength for the community as a whole. Such a vision of the future of the community uniting officials together from different parts of the community brings the organizations into a new future.

Activists

Women activists are a group of community workers that are very much influenced by the Asian American Movement that swept this country in the late 1960's and early 1970's. This movement was a source in molding the women activists who were then college students. Their consciousness as a separate ethnic community was linked to the large social forces in American society during this period; particularly the student movement, the anti-war movement and the Civil Rights Movement and the movement opposing the foreign policy of the United States government toward Asia in the 1960's (Kuo, 1977:62). Although the Asian American Movement came later than the Civil Rights Movement, the main thrust of this movement was due to the events that took place in the Vietnam War in the 1970's. However, the movement did not die when the war ended. The participants transferred their involvement to the community. Community activists view Chinatown as a product of American policies of exploiting Asians by excluding them from political participation and denying them adequate facilities and services in the community (Wang, 1972). Thus, community organizations that developed in the mid-1970's in this community could be seen as a political organization to find solutions for pressing social issues in Chinatown (Kuo, 1977:62).

Community activists interviewed, who experienced and identified with the Asian-American Movement in giving them strength in their community work, are mostly American-born and identify themselves as working-class Chinese-Americans. Although none of the community activists mentioned Cheng-tu Wu's (1972) work, Chink!, I find it

75

noteworthy; for it expresses the overall view of community activists who were interviewed. Wu awakens Asian-American consciousness by saying that Asians here should fight for equal rights, and he stresses the importance of Chinese community as a place to begin in advocating equality issues and the development of leadership in the community. Community activists for the most part are well-educated in Marxist ideology and this motivates their concern with equal rights. Their ideology convinces them that the most important goal in advocating equal rights for Chinese people is to bring a people-empowered organization into the community.

In order to understand the movement and the inspiration that involvement brings to these women activists, the following section introduces two community activists who have been active since the past ten years in the community. Both were influenced by the Asian-American Movement in college. Each has her own working style and commitment. Each is a leader in her own sphere.

Candice: Grass-roots Organizer

Candice is married. Both she and her husband work in the Chinese Progressive, Incorporated organization in B Street. When I first visited the place, it struck me as odd because I was used to seeing modern facilities and equipment and more workers. The first thing that I saw in the organization was a large room that ran from the front to the back with no partition. The place had no heat. Candice told me that the Chinese Progressive, Inc. only operates on the weekends: Friday night, Saturday and Sunday. Classes and recreational activities are run on the weekends because that is when the people in the community have free time. The rest of the week the organization is closed. That explained why there was no heat, and Candice was the only one that I met.

Candice began talking about her family background. She was born in New York and, like many community activists, she comes from a working-class family and identifies with the community. She first talked about her family:

76

My father did a lot of different kinds of work. He worked in
Chinese restaurants....I grew up with Chinese as my first language and I didn't learn English until I went to school, but
in my house we were only allowed to speak Chinese when I was
growing up.

The consciousness of herself as being different began early during her school age. She

said:

I always felt that there was discrimination against me, or
people had certain stereotype of me because I was Chinese
and I certainly felt that for my parents. They had a very
hard life and a lot of that was because how people treated
Chinese.

This difference that she felt is also felt by other community activists who grew up in

Chinese community and experienced working-class poverty. So that even when they went

to college, they consider themselves a group apart.

The Asian-American Movement heightened their unique situation. What they indivi-

dually felt began to be discussed openly with other Chinese and Asian-Americans who

felt that it was time for a change, and the place to start was on campus. Candice ex-

plained the Asian-American Movement and what she did on campus in Northville:

I was in school from 1968 to 1972....In 1970, the U.S. in-
vaded Cambodia and extended the war from Vietnam to include
Cambodia. Nationwide, campuses went on strike. Blumery
[the college's name] went on an optional strike. Some students continued to go to classes, but students who wanted to
work against the war will have a chance to complete the classes they lost....[laugh] you know, you won't be kicked out of
school for it.

A group of Asians began to form and they became active on campus. She said:

A group started forming in Northville called the Greater Northville Asian Alliance....Different people who wanted to address
the war and...something that Asians had to say about the war...
because it was being fought in Asia....

Apart from being active in anti-war activities, these activists also demanded that

Asian-American studies be offered and they started to work to change the admission

77

policy for minority students. However, Candice emphasized that the significance of
the organization was to involve student activists directly with community work. She
said:

> We...the group that was the Asian Alliance...were the first one
> in Chinatown to demonstrate against Ace University in 1971.

This direct participation in the community brought a significant change in her life.
She said:

> ...identifying with the community is very important because I
> think what I started to understand in college really comes into
> reality when I work in the community...how the Chinese [should]
> exist in collective existence...the Chinese can say: I can go to
> college, I can do this, I can do that...but actually that's not
> true because they put the Japanese-Americans in concentration
> camps who were being Japanese-Americans and you could be a mer-
> chant, you could have a Ph.D...and I think that's the same for
> Chinese that we exist as a group and if we don't help each other
> then...everybody helps themselves, our people don't advance.

Community activists perceive community work as a collective political work. The community worker is striving towards a new society. Candice explained:

> I think for Chinese to speak out and to fight for their lives,
> is progress for the whole society. It's not like Chinese
> against whites, I think it is making the society more equitable.

A progressive society is defined as one where everyone is working towards a more united
goal. For this reason, community activists use the term, "progressive." The goal that
community activists are fighting for is equality. It is the key and fundamental concept and ideology in the progressive movement that developed out of the Asian-American
Movement that affects Asian-Americans in the 1970's. Candice explained the progressive
philosophy of community activists:

> I think basically, Chinese people are striving for equality
> and for more control of their lives. I think it will take
> many different forms...at different times. We can fight
> more for certain things...it includes things like the right
> to own our own community, which we're not realizing right
> now...

The community activists are working towards this particular goal by establishing
organizations that are grass-roots, increasing the participation among community people

in taking up social issues that community service agencies are not in the position to do, such as busing and land encroachment.

The majority of community activists work full time in the community. Candice and other community activists that I have come to know do not want to obtain employment outside the community. Having been brought up in the community, they have returned, even though their college degree could earn them a position outside the community and in private industries that could give them a higher living standard. Candice works in the day-care center of the community, and spend most of her time working with parents, teachers and tenants. Like other activists, her personal life and community work are tightly interwined. Activists' jobs are related to community work, their friends are community people, and their colleagues are organized around community issues. On weekends, they socialize among friends, colleagues, and also community people. The grass-roots organization opened only on weekends provides many of these community activists with a place to specialize and work with the community people without any clear separation between their community work and their personal lives.

Unlike the community workers who work and belong to the community service organizations, the activists' community work is more directly political. Demonstration and public protest and strategies that community workers have learned to make their demands known, rather than being passive recipients of American society. Their demands change with time, but always identify with community people and Asian-American needs. In looking at different issues that they work on, one sees that the activists deal with education, housing, unionization, and bettering the social life of the community people. The activists, though involved in different grass-roots organizations, provide help to other community workers whenever necessary. Because their definition of goals and purposes in these grass-roots organizations is broad and their community work on issues is varied, many community workers who are not activists cannot understand what the activists are trying to do. Many community workers are surprised that these

79

grass-roots organizations have continued to survive in the community for five years or more, and that community people participate in these organizations. As for the activists, their goal is self-defined, and the work is for the Chinese people in the community, not primarily for community organizations. Their working organization serves as a location for different Asian-Americans to meet and exchange ideas, plans, visions and is a political as well as a social place where community people are welcomed.

Ying: A Community Activist and Feminist

Ying is part of the Asian-American Movement, but unlike Candice who was brought up on the East Coast, Ying was brought up on the West Coast where the Asian-American Movement was an even larger movement on major college campuses. Ying came to Northville four years ago to continue her graduate study. While pursuing her doctorate in psychology, Ying works part time in the health center. When I interviewed Ying at home, she first talked about her family background and how the West Coast's Asian-American Movement changed her life. Ying began:

> I grew up in San Francisco's Chinatown. I live there for
> seventeen years...when I got involved it was in Bee Univer-
> sity with the Asian-American women's group. It was the
> first group that started in the nation and it was a course
> that was taught at the university under the Asian-American
> Studies. There was the third world movement in...Nick
> College in San Francisco and we just rallied...

The women's group influenced and changed her whole life. She said:

> The women's group really helped to consolidate my political
> perspective, and the kind of activities that I could do for
> the community. That was the base line that you have to un-
> derstand...Prior to that I didn't realize that it was
> meaningful, and I didn't know what to do with my life and
> career....I really want to do more, I didn't find things
> very challenging, the women's group really helped to conso-
> lidate that for me by allowing me to be involved intensely
> in politics with theory-buildings with Asian Studies.

Moreover, the women's group also paved the way for community participation that has been a part of her life for more than ten years. She related

We got involved with community issues like housing and
labor,...garment-sewing factories, and factory owners;
and we did a lot of community-based support....I remember...my mother has always been a seamstress and she
worked for a factory that we were involved with because
they were discriminating against minorities and they
weren't paying them enough money. They were paying
them minimum wage. I remember going to the factory
and picketing....[laugh] but she kind of supported that
too, because I talked to her about it.

For Ying, being an activist comes from long years of seeing the community as a

place to work when she finished college. Although her women's group had disintegrat-

ed and she moved out East to continue her graduate study, her past experiences and

background have strongly imprinted her outlook of life.

For Ying, moving here and going to school does not mean that she has stopped doing

community work. Her experiences in the Asian-American Movement has motivated her in

participating in two organizations. One is grass-roots and the other is a community-

service organization. At the same time, she works part time in the community. Poli-

tical activism is still very important in her life:

We needed to do more for the community because I grew
up there [Chinatown], I knew what my mother had to go
through and what I had to go through, and the fact is,
we need to organize and have political power and advocate for our own community. So, that's what my own perspective is, and everything I do, even the career, the
psychology I do, is almost community work because it's
so individual-oriented....I still help people.

Activists shared common experiences with community people while growing and by

working within the community, their personal interests and lives remain closely a-

ligned with the community. Unlike professionals, who leave the community after their

day is over, community activists stay on to participate in another realm of commu-

nity involvement. Even though most of them do not live in Chinatown, because of

their working-class background, they feel a comfort and a sense of belonging in the

community.

81

Again, like Candice, Ying emphasized unity, equality and helping one another. To her, community work means:

> ...supporting each other; working with groups; building lea-
> dership with other people and I think that everyone has the
> responsibility to develop that...
> I believe in working in the community to get somewhere, to
> achieve growth and education, not just politically [but]
> personally.

The Commitment of the Activists

Community activists' interests are diverse. Officials only work on specific interests like education or health care. Community activists have wider interests, even
though their main interest remains helping and supporting people's demands and concerns. To do this, activists do not think expertise in a certain area is important as
the ability to work with people and help them develop their strength and skills.

These community activists feel that the Asian-American Movement expanded their personal lives in that they focus their community work, personal life and career/job on
one goal. There is no clear distinction as to where one activity begins or ends. The
movement gave them strength and hope to work for the people but also for the community. They are not concerned with providing services but with coalescing the community
into a grass-roots power-base that can agitate for equality and unity.

Conclusion

Community work encompasses a variety of activities, and degrees of involvement on
issues of social, educational, financial, cultural, and political importance to the
Chinese community. The four subtypes of community workers' involvement in Northville
Chinatown in this chapter enable us to better comprehend the community workers' activities, and enable us to understand how their background influences the amount of commitment and attachment to the community. The four subtypes are also a product of the

82

historical events and crises that emerged in the community. When I mentioned these subtypes of community workers to my interviewees, they were aware that such different groups existed, and perceived the subtypes: volunteers, professionals, officials, and activists, to be derived from and reflect the historical precedence of community development over the past forty years in Northville Chinatown. In the beginning, there were volunteers that devoted their time to helping community people with problems. When the conditions of Chinatown became overwhelming for the volunteers to handle, the professionals and officials (especially the Old Vanguards) emerged in the late 1960's and early 1970's to establish the human service organizations. In the mid-1970's, the activists became visible in the community, bringing with them their experiences of the Asian-American Movement and grass-roots organizing.

In realizing the importance of subtypes that exist among community workers, one sees that their differences also form the basis of conflict that exists in the community. Such conflict comes from differences in personal as well as political orientation, that determine principles and goals for community work. For example, the activists take a political stand, using community work as a tool for advocating equality and unity, and visibly publicizing problems that exist in Chinatown. The professionals, on the other hand, prefer to work within the political system to get what they want (resources and funding) for the community, rather than changing (advocating) the features. All these different orientations make up a community full of struggles, concerns, and difficulties as well as accomplishments.

The subtypes also categorize the different ways in which women community workers get involved, and how they see their professional and private commitments in relation to community participation. Although subtype formulation is an analytical device that serves to clarify the difference and degrees of commitment, it is not a rigid categorization, and women's changing involvement depends on where they are in their life cycle. In cases of the volunteers interviewed, the married volunteers' time was taken up with their family; however, when their children enrolled in school, many of these women become involved with educational issues, such as Ann in this chapter. Ming represents another example where her involvement remains less than other community workers because of her busy schoolwork. When she graduates, she will become more involved with the community.

Women's involvement also depends greatly on how they relate their careers to community work. Lynn, for example, used to be a teacher. Her involvement with educational interests brought her to the Chinese community school. Now that she has changed her career and is a legal assistant dealing with community people, however, her interest lies with legal cases. Thus, she is looking into the Housing and Land Association as a place to be involved in. Since community workers strive for changes that better the community, it is not possible that they remain rigid in doing one type of community work. Their selection of priorities and interests, backed by their commitment, enables them to move from one type of activity to another. This increases the cohesion, co-operation and unity that all community workers are looking for. Nevertheless, the subtypes remain as a beginning identifier for their involvement in the community.

Of the thirty-two community workers that were interviewed and subtyped, nineteen are either originally from different parts of the country or from Asia. These community workers who first came to study and work in Northville stayed to work in the community and brought with them enriching knowledge, new orientations and energy. These "outsiders," born and raised outside of Northville, are scattered among the volunteers, officials, professionals and activists. They are just as dedicated as community workers who were brought up in Northville.

In talking with women community workers and seeing them within the subtypes context, one notices clear-cut differences in terms of how these women spend their private and public lives. Though professionals and volunteers are similar in separating

84

community involvement and their personal lives, they have differing commitments. The commitment of volunteers is minimal compared to professionals, officials and activists in that they see community work as "doing something useful" but in a less committed way due to priorities of children and family as well as work or school that take them away from full commitment in the community. The professionals have taken jobs that they realize are important in the community. Although they are qualified and could be paid more working outside of the community, they prefer to stay. However, there is a limit in what they can give because their human service jobs are not easy. Professionals sometimes have to do more than what they are assigned to do, thus, they react by keeping a stringent distance between their private and public lives. There are professionals that do more by becoming officials, thereby showing that they do not differentiate between working and being involved in the community. Four of the officials on the school board in Chinatown are professional staff of the health center. A day's work and a night's meeting makes them stay in the community longer than the average professionals. Both officials and activists spend more time in the community than volunteers. In addition to their full time jobs, they all spend many weeknights attending board, committee, ad hoc committee and emergency meetings, and tend to make less of a distinction between work and social activities. Their commitment and devotion is maximum compared to the volunteers, and the responsibility of handling crises, policies, and planning of programs, and events requires much time and makes community involvement their priority. This is exemplified in the work officials like Jade and Jean do as well as those done by activists like Ying and Candice. This chapter provides inside stories and experiences from the four groups of community workers that explain their commitment to the community.

CHAPTER IV   NETWORKING

In order for community workers to work effectively together, they should share the same goals and visions. Thus, they are close-knit and know each other well. Their main concern is maintaining their commitment to serve the Chinese community and dedicating their time and effort in making impossible dreams come true.

Social linkages or social networks emerged out of a high degree of social interaction or contacts among community workers. A social network here is defined as a "specific set of linkages among a defined set of persons, with the...property that the characteristics of these linkages as a whole may be used to interpret the social behavior of the persons involved" (Mitchell, 1969:2). The women community workers who worked together in the community know the importance of ties that bind their common interests. In addition, these ties enable them to maintain and support each other's work and strengthen their conviction of doing community work and serving the Chinese community. Without such linkages in the community, the work that these community workers do becomes difficult and inefficient, and their aims, interests, goals and achievements are not fulfilled. This chapter examines the historical development of the ties women community workers have with one another, the types of networks volunteers, officials, professionals and activists forge with one another and the usefulness of direct and indirect linkages in community work.

The community, even though located in an urban area, is not impersonal, transitory and segmented (Wirth, 1938:12). Rather, all persons are directly or indirectly linked to each other. The community workers who forged these linkages constantly maintained them, knowing full well that social networks are the mobilizing force in the Chinese community.

86

Traditional Ties

We always exclaim, "Oh, what a small world" when we discover that a friend of ours is also a friend's friend or relative. It is often surprising, especially when we knew this friend for a long time, but did not know of such close linkage. It is re-assuring too, to discover such a link when one is in a foreign environment. Natural-ly, this person will receive a warm welcome because of the linkages that are revealed. According to Stanley Milgram (1969), everyone in the world may be linked to everyone else through indirect acquaintanceship paths with an average length of five. This ac-quaintanceship path is even more direct when looking at the traditional linkages in the Chinese community. Historically, the Chinese community is known to be close-knit. Katherine, a community worker born in Northville, revealed that in the old days, every-one knew everyone else in the community; but when she walks down Chinatown today, she does not know a soul. Such traditional ties are forged among kin and it is most im-portant that these close kin maintain such ties.

Stanford Lyman (1974:17) points out in his study of the Chinese American that, "Overseas Chinese are organized not only in terms of clan-designating surnames but also according to place of origin and spoken dialect." Chinese people called this type of organization as "hui-kuan." Similarly, Siu (1953:188-209) notes that it was quite common among Chinese immigrants to transfer resources between relatives in the host society and the homeland. And Ivan Light (1973) in his study of the Chinese business enterprise finds that rotating credit associations among Chinese are main-tained by regional and kinship ties which enables capital to be generated for ethnic enterprise. These studies suggest that networking in the Chinese community is impor-tant not only in bringing their kin over to the United States and handling family and personal matters but also in celebrating events of the community such as the Chinese

87

New Year, the opening of a new restaurant, or even a full-month (Mun-yi) banquet celebration of a one-month-old baby thrown by the family.

The hui-kuan is centered around kinship and the belief that when one needs help,
it is proper to go to close kin. This is a Chinese custom that is observed even today.
Such linkages are very important to maintain. When one is looking for a job, one pass-
es the word to close kin first before getting in touch with friends. According to
Peter Li (1977:486), job assistance by relatives in many cases extends to actually
working for relatives. In a survey that he did in the Chicago area with 450 Chinese,
Li found that 67% of them actually worked for relatives for a period of time. This is
unlikely to be found among Americans, where indirect linkages through contacts among
friends remain the most important resource in getting a job (Granovetter, 1973; Jacobson, 1975).

Such close kinship is also important to women, but that kinship is family oriented.
Help in caring for the children, decisions regarding the coming and going of relatives
and matters related to matchmaking are the domains of women.

The extension of networks and ties has undergone moderate changes even though kinship ties still reamin important. Women now reach out to non-kin ties and it is possible to do so, especially if they do community work. Even after women and their families move out to the suburbs, coming back to visit the community is a common pattern.
They look up friends, and observe events and celebrations in Chinatown. Meeting in
Chinatown is the first step in forging new ties and maintaining old ones.

The Northville Chinese Women's Club and later, the Northville Chinese Life-Enrichment Committee Center are two such organizations that are opened to women to meet regularly in Chinatown. These organizations cut across the kinship lines and not only
enable women community workers to advance their work but also maintain the close ties
they have in Chinatown.

Nevertheless, recognition of the traditional family and kinship ties still remain

important. One incident that reminds me of such traditional kin networks was the recent tenth anniversary banquet held by the health center. Millie, a community worker
who works with me on the health board renewed links with her distant uncle (the chairman of CCBA) that enabled the banquet to be held at the restaurant he owns. She was
able to get him to write letters of support and recommendation to the other restaurant owners to make this fundraising banquet a success. These connections are still
significant even though community organizations promote networking of community workers beyond kin boundaries.

Networking Among Women

An illustration of the direct linkages among the thirty-two community workers are
shown in the following figure (Figure 4, page 90). The straight lines from one end
to another indicate the direct linkages that community workers have with one another,
as revealed by the mention of names that are close friends and colleagues or important
source-person to contact. To give an example, we can look at No. 1, who is Millie, an
official who works on the health board. She is directly linked with Nos. 2, 17, and
26 (see Appendix A for names), for they all belong to the same board in the health
agency and meet frequently during the board and committee meetings. At the same time,
Millie (No. 1) went to school with her friends who are activists in the Chinese community, and she still maintains relationships with Nos. 5, 13 and 28 and sees them at a
women's support group at least once a month. In the case of Millie, her contact is
wider than, say No. 31, Cecilia, that joined only one suburban organization. Moreover,
Millie also sits on another board in the Chinese community and knows Nos. 4 and 7
through their joint membership in the center of adult education. Millie is an example
of the networking of women community workers who work inside Chinatown. However, there
are others who work outside of Chinatown as well, and this type of linkage is just as
important.

89

Figure 3   Social Linkages of the Women Community Workers

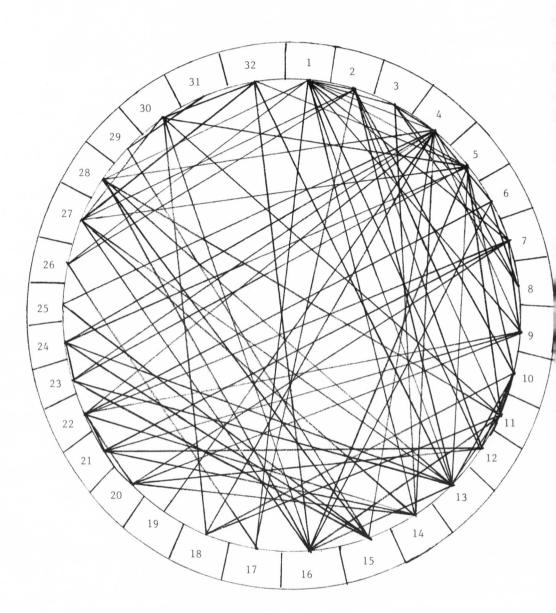

I called outside linkages to the Chinese community as source-persons. In figure
, Cleo (No. 6), Katherine (No. 7), Mimi (No. 9), and Heather (No. 22) are all source-
ersons who work in private corporations and public agencies and are familiar with
undraising, grant proposal policies and have contacts in private and public founda-
ions. These are the community workers who play major roles behind the scene and are
ware of their roles. These source-persons are well-informed about the latest policy
hanges and new information resources and can relate relevant information to the com-
unity workers in the Chinese community. The source-persons and their linkages to
hinatown are strengthened by the similar backgrounds and common interests that these
ommunity workers share.

As community workers linked with others directly, it is plausible to break down
ne subtypes of community workers and look at the number of linkages each subtype
as with other community workers. Table 1 shows the number of linkages each subtype
f community workers have with one another.

Table 1   Linkages of Subtypes of Community Workers

Volunteers		# of linkages		Professionals		# of linkages
Ann	(N.15)	7		Ling	(N. 3)	5
Marge	(N.27)	5		Woo	(N. 4)	11
Ruby	(N.25)	2		Angie	(N.12)	4
Heather	(N.22)	7		Aline	(N.14)	6
Jane	(N.29)	2		Nancy	(N.20)	4
Mink	(N.32)	5		Mao-lin	(N.21)	6
Cecilia	(N.31)	1		Lucille	(N.24)	2
Natalie	(N.30)	5		Nettie	(N.19)	1
		34				39

Officials		# of linkages		Activists		# of linkages
Millie	(N. 1)	11		*Jade	(N. 2)	6
Cleo	(N. 6)	4		Candice	(N. 5)	9
Katherine	(N. 7)	4		*Lynn	(N.10)	6
Jean	(N. 8)	2		*Ying	(N.11)	7
Mimi	(N. 9)	5		Emily	(N.13)	7
Geraldine	(N.26)	2		Di	(N.16)	7
Lily	(N.18)	4		Su-ling	(N.23)	4
Annette	(N.17)	2		San-San	(N.28)	7
		34				53

* also board members (Officials) of
  community organizations

Clearly, the activist community workers have the most network linkages in the community. Since activists work with different people from grass-roots organizations to professionals, they bring with them different contacts from teachers and musicians to lawyers. Also, in this group, Jade, Lynn and Ying are members of the community organizations' board of directors, and they bring with them the ideology and skills of grass-roots organizing as well as leadership skills, and could be called the "young bloods" of officials. The group or subtype that has the next highest number of linkages of the professionals since they, like the activists, spend a lot of time in the community. The volunteers and the officials have the same amount of linkages, but since officials usually have connections and contacts with suburban and outside private and public agencies, these contacts prove useful in bringing new resources, skills, and information into community organizations they serve. This is similar to volunteers who may not participate at full capacity; however, they are linkages with outside associations and may prove to be the most resourceful group to get in touch with for community crises as well as events.

The great amount of time spent on interaction, simultaneously benefits problem-solving and strengthens ties of the individuals involved. Networks foster a unique friendship among community workers that strengthens and intensifies joint efforts to deal with difficult situations and work in the community. This could be said about the banquet committee in the health center. Because of the common interest that the committee members have, the sentiment was to make the banquet a success. Banquet committee members worked together and met practically every weekend to solicit nearby restaurants and private corporations and met again on weeknights to coordinate the details of the banquet.

Time is an important element in strengthening such ties in the community. The more time one spends with one anther, both through difficult and easy periods of events, the more direct and strong their linkages are. It is, in addition, easier for the community workers to relate to one another and give support. Through such closeness, one can better understand the working style of another and avoid conflict.

Women community workers not only share close working relationships but also certain sentiments that are not present among men community workers. I can remember one particular night when the banquet chairperson, Eileen, called me around midnight to share her disagreement with certain decisions. Her emotional outburst was shared by Millie and me in a candid interaction that resulted from our close ties and would not have been feasible with others. As Mark Granovetter (1973:1361) points out, "the strength of a tie is a combination of the amount of time, the emotional

93

intensity, the intimacy and the reciprocal services which characterize the tie."
This is exemplified frequently by the common emotional feelings that are easily expressed among the women community workers who are overworked sometimes and must perform under pressure. Such a unique communication and sharing among community workers
are considered to be exclusively understood by fellow network members. This is discussed in detail in Chapter Six, where differences of working style among men and women community workers point out the role women community workers play in the community.

The Uses of Networking in the Community

Apart from direct linkages, source-person linkages and the high degree of linkages shared by different subtypes of community workers, there are also indirect
linkages that are essential to the world of community workers. "Weak ties" (Granovetter, 1973) are just as important as strong ties in the community. For instance,
when Millie (No. 1) called me for information about who to contact in getting a
mailing list of the suburban Chinese organizations in Northville, I immediately
mentioned Ann (No. 15) who works for the Chinese community's newspaper, Dragon Boat.
Millie recalled that she somehow knew Ann and remembered that she contacted Ann
when she did an article on a fundraising event of the Adult Education center and
had spoken to her. So I gave Millie Ann's phone number and Millie obtained names
and information that she needed. The weak tie between Millie (No. 1) and Ann (No.15)
was forged through a middle person (Ego, or the author in this case). The following diagram shows such a weak tie between No. 1 and No. 15 in obtaining and sharing
important information. Under the circumstances, they will not be maintaining the
relationship unless repeated contacts are made. The tie between No. 1 and No. 15
will remain weak.

94

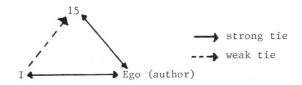

15

I ◄————————► Ego (author)

————► strong tie

- - -► weak tie

The first use of network linkages is to gain access to information that is relevant to women's work in the community. Mitchell (1969:36) points out such a linkage
that relates the flow of communication through networks is called a communication-set
network. Community workers provide indirect access to a greater diversity of resources than more socially homogeneous ties (Granovetter, 1973), and since each individual is a member of a unique personal network, membership in these networks serves
to connect a number of social circles (Craven and Wellman, 1973). Millie and Ann
provide the case in point. Millie's social circle is centered within the community;
whereas Ann's social circle is centered around the suburban areas. Because of the
information Millie needs, and the information suburban organizations may want to know
about community organizations, the channels are opened by such individuals for ideas
and information. Thus, community workers spend an enormous amount of time and effort
in reaching new network linkages that may be useful (potential links) as well as
maintaining strong linkages in their work.

A second use of linkages is to reinforce the values and goals that community workers maintain among their own groups. Bott (1957:60) points out that:

> When many of the people a person knows interact with one
> another, that is when the person's network is close-knit,
> the members of his network tend to reach consensus of
> norms that they exert consistent informal pressure on
> one another to conform.

In the community, community workers know who to approach for the relevant information
they need for their work. Community workers called this "touching base." Ling, an
administrator in the adult education agency, told me that frequently they meet each
other in their work:

> At these meetings, we say, 'Are you still around, are your
> programs....fine, we're doing this, and you're doing that.'
> Calling for letter of support occasionally, so there is
> that willingness even though we're all busy with our own
> sphere of interest. There wasn't resistance to lending...
> a hand for creating new programs.

Such frequent contact among the agencies also lessens duplication of each other's

program and policies. The general consensus here is to lessen competition with one

another to avoid creating bad feelings. Community organizations will regularly write

a letter to support or recommend a new program for another, as an expression of mutual

support in the hope that someday the favor will be returned. Agencies also share

grant information and if one agency is interested in getting the same grant as anoth-

er, then they will negotiate and reach a compromise. Usually, if this happens, both

agencies will join in a grant proposal to ask for a larger amount of money than pre-

viously planned by the agency alone. The chances are sometimes brighter for the two

agencies together than doing it alone and fighting against each other in a "disunity"

that community workers frown upon.

Source-persons, as I have mentioned earlier, are important in community work; and

everyone of the community workers at one time or another is a source-person. A

source-person is located in various positions of the organizational structures in the

community as well as outside of the community. These connections may at some point

be important because of certain knowledge these source-persons may bring into the

community, from finding a job to looking at certain grants that may be available.

Unfortunately, because of these outside linkages, not many source-persons can be di-

rectly involved in the community organization. This happened to Katherine who had

to resign from the board of an agency that she once founded. She said:

> It's a conflict of interest. That is actually a basic
> problem for people like me, who are in the federal gov-
> ernment. Because so many programs are funded by the
> federal government, you have to make sure you don't
> have a conflict of interest.

Nevertheless, she still maintains her ties with community workers that she came to know during her work in the community. She said, "I am sort of a bridge between them and what I am doing in my work and I still like to provide help whenever there is a need to do so."

What strikes me the most about networking among women community workers is that there is little rivalry among women I interviewed and observed in the community setting. There is a general feeling of willingness to help and share important information when community workers are approached. Thus, women community workers are potential links because of their willingness to be open and to co-operate and share relevant information. It is not rare to hear that it is a great achievement to establish such important links. Jean, for example, mentioned to me her connections. She said:

> My biggest achievement for the community is the fact that
> I have so many contacts and I can be of so much help to
> the people.

The greatest difficulty of networking is extending it nationally to outsiders. Usually this takes a lot of traveling and frequent attendance at national conferences. This could be said about sociologists who take time to attend the sociological conferences nationwide and worldwide, just as professional community workers attend government conferences to keep informed about policy changes and opportunities and also make contacts. Lily is such a person and unlike her colleagues, she takes time to go out of her way to attend every educational conference that she hears of. She also submits papers and reports for presentation at national conferences so that she can seek advice and input from other public school administrators throughout the country. She said:

> I have won national recognition among...educators, spe-
> cifically, Asians...and...then I realized that I can ex-
> pand on that level. I could write curriculum and I have
> a few published which are used by the school system,
> even though the teachers here don't know it....[laugh]

She commented on her achievements and realization of such linkages in the following manner:

97

> I have personally set up a close network, so that I can
> have names at my fingertips, practically any instance
> that arises from any community concerns. For example...
> we're losing Asian teachers in the regular programs, not
> bi-lingual teachers. but in the regular programs. I call-
> ed Washington, and I got the Asian-Pacific concerned staff
> to write a letter of support. Those are the kinds of con-
> tact that are benefitting my community work even though
> they are built on a nationwide basis.

Then, there are others who sit on private foundations that are important source-per-

sons. Their willingness to give advice to community workers who are looking for

funds is most valuable during such "hard times" when federal funds are cut severely.

Cleo is such a person since she was promoted to work at corporate-giving department

of a large corporation in Northville. She told me of her realization of such linkage

in the following interview:

> Most of the community relations effort has to do with the
> wide community, but it also allows me to do something for
> Chinatown, small things...yes, at least I am in the posi-
> tion to do that. Some of that.

In addition, she talked about this networking linkage among other corporate and

foundation agencies. She said:

> ...and I am also in the networking position. I can be with
> other people in the corporate community and represent...the
> Chinese community, the Chinese interests, the Chinese needs
> and provide input. These are what I meant by different levels.

Overall, she said of her networking potential in the following way:

> My contacts, my networking is wider, much wider and has a
> much better impact. It's a very formal network and all of
> us are either with a foundation or with a company that makes
> corporate contributions. I'm the only Chinese person there.
> There's probably other Chinese women and men in these kinds
> of positions and some of them, I think people like Heather
> or Mr. C, [are] conscious about that role, and I think it's
> important. And I took the responsibility in my involvement.

The woman community worker whom Cleo mentioned, Heather, sits on major foundations'

boards in Northville, and she was very helpful in giving me a two-page list of found-

ations that she is involved with. When I counted the number of foundations that

she is involved on the board level, the total number was twelve. This number shocked

me, but with her habit of working sixteen hours a day for more than twenty years,
Heather is truly an active community worker.

Networking among women community workers has expanded to community-, city- and
national-levels. The public role of Chinese women has widened by expanding the traditional ties of women. A third use of networking is to recruit new community
workers to be officials, professionals, activists and volunteers. This not only widens
the networks women forged in the community but also provides new people with fresh
ideas, skills, experiences and energy. Concerned community workers have always wanted
to involve new people into the community, whether Chinese students or workers search-
ing for their identity or a training ground, the community is a place to start.

It is often discussed during board and small committee meetings that one has a
responsibility to reach out to people outside the community organization, whether in
soliciting funds, in filling positions of officials and professionals that are vacant,
or asking in friends to help out with community events. It is not a compulsory policy
that every community worker has to follow, but those who are concerned about vacan-
cies want to ensure that there will be others to join the community organizations.
In such cases, community workers' personal networks become very useful. It is also
important in the recruitment process to bring in new members so that other community
workers who remain during crisis after crisis do not burnout too soon.

A fourth use in networking is to mobilize forces in the community. Adrian Mayer
(1966) has called this type of networking "action-type," that is, it is an instru-
mentally-activated personal network to achieve desired ends. In the past, the network among teachers and parents was useful. The parents, for instance Jane (No.
29), Cecilia (No. 31) and Ann (No. 15) have constantly kept in touch with one another
even though they all live in different parts of the suburbs outside Northville. Ann
(No. 15) also is a close friend of Su-ling, who works in the Parents Association in
the Chinese community. Their concerns for bi-lingual education and public school

99

policy changes are relayed by Ann to Su-ling, who recently became a public school teacher. When the busing issue became a community issue in the mid-1970's, parents inside and outside the community demanded a two-day boycott. The parents got in touch with one another through the network of suburban parents and city parents, and both Ann and Su-ling played a major role in organizing this united action. Through other teachers, Su-ling also has become friends with Emily (No. 13), who has a long history of activism both in college and in the community. She not only organized the parents in her personal network but also Chinese teachers throughout Northville. The two-day boycott became a success when parents' demands as well as teachers' demand for better security for Chinese school children was met by public school superintendent and officials.

Finally, networking is useful in providing community workers with support and encouragement. Ying, an official, called this the social element in working in the community. She pointed out the importance of giving such support. She said:

> I think that the social element is really important in
> order to maintain people's work in the community. It
> doesn't mean that you have to socialize a lot. It just
> means that you got the social element in you to [give
> to] people, it gets them onto something like...giving
> them a lot of support and encouragement and...motivation.

This is a very important and useful strategy in staying committed and not burning out at the same time. Moreover, it gives community workers a sense of achievement that is appreciated by their friends and co-workers. Ying continued:

> I feel that the people I got on the board are friends
> and people are closer to me after working with me that
> is the way to keep all of us going....

This type of support is necessary when one spends the great amount of one's time in the community.

Community workers who treat each other as friends extend their linkages to a personal level. Mao-lin, who is now in Hong Kong, told me before she left:

> I think one of the great achievements is that I made
> a lot of friends.
> This maybe...not totally related but once I thought
> of this question. People say to me: Well, what would
> you like people to remember you? And I always like to
> say, if anything I like people to remember me...as a
> friend.

Mao-lin appeared in the Chinese opera in Northville as a classical actress. She not only is well-versed in the Chinese art of singing and acting but also produces educational programs for children on public television.

One thing that people enjoy doing community work is the circle of friends they made in the community. Community workers that have used and benefitted from such a network of friends value it very much and it is one of the most remembered souvenirs of community work and the hardest to leave.

The environment outside the community is hostile in that it sometimes produces conflict that interferes with networking. A word of caution here is that not all linkages are beneficial and useful, and one has to be selective before proceeding head on to acquire more and more linkages in places that may prove to be a waste of time and energy. As a community worker, one has to be extremely cautious in the world of community work. The following two incidents that happened in a community organization that I was involved in relate the importance of selectivity. Networking takes time before it is an effective strategy to be used by community workers.

One incident happened earlier in 1982 when a working committee was set up for an anniversary celebration that was to be held later that year. Since the plan was a fundraising banquet event, there was a discussion about putting a group of potential fundgivers onto a honorary body that would preside over the banquet day. The selection process became the most important, and community workers had to check out the backgrounds of potential benefactors before inviting them into the honorary body. One of the identifying criteria was whether the fundgiver was a pro-China or Pro-Taiwan individual. Since inviting a pro-China individual might cause some discomfort, because the banquet would be held at a pro-Taiwan owner's restaurant, it was decided to proceed with care. This is an eye-opening experience for a lot of American-born Chinese who are not aware of this division in the community.

The second incident happened to a community worker not very long ago. This community worker, whom I call "Z" was looking for an administrative position around Northville and happened to talk to Ace University Hospital in Chinatown about the job position. It was only a search interview with no intention on the part of this particular community worker to apply. Z only sought information about the job market. Somehow, word leaked out to the community workers within the official level and Z was reprimanded severely. Z, on his part was furious that the community workers did not understand his circumstances, that he had not applied for any position but was only seeking input about the administrative job market during hard times. However, community workers feel that Ace University Hospital is an "enemy " of the community since there is a long history of land encroachment, and if such linkage between Z and Ace is continued, Z will have to resign on the grounds of conflict of interest. The incident sanctioned a break on Z's contact with the university because according to the community workers, his contact was "not the right kind."

These two incidents have not only cautioned new members but also reinforced certain unwritten guidelines in the world of community work: that delicate balance and selectivity have to be exercised by individuals on the interest of the general community. No one knows in advance about these conflicts that interfere with networking unless through experience in doing community work and being in the community for a period of time. Such touchy subjects are too uncomfortable for community workers to discuss during interviews.

Overall, the links between individuals and community enable the exchange of ideas and the co-ordinating and planning of activities so that the community as a whole becomes strengthened through the ties community workers have established on the

personal as well as professional levels. Network linkage, once centered around kinship and family ties, are now moving to wider ties that are centered around friends,
colleagues, and people whom community workers meet during their work and national
conferences. Network linkage is used extensively for obtaining information, rein-
forcing existing goals and values, recruiting new workers, mobilizing the community,
and providing support and encouragement. Potential, indirect, and direct linkages,
and ties are all essential whenever there is a need to re-establish and plan community organizations' events as well as handling crises. In order to maintain such
force in the community, networking must be constantly reinforced by community workers aided by telephone and ties extended to individuals that live and work outside
the community and nationwide. Thus, linkages and networks of the community workers
are a strategic mechanism that pull activists and the Chinese people together.

CHAPTER V   HARD WORK

According to the women community workers, community work is not an easy job. It
is demanding and stressful, but community workers come to accept these conditions as
a challenge. These women are not looking for a glamourous job in the community with
high-paying salary and promotions. The ultimate reason that they remain in the community and do not go in search of another job is their concern for the community and
issues as well as the growth of their organizations. This chapter focuses on the
major difficulties of community work as well as the strengths women must develop in
order to endure and work out problems. The areas of difficulties center around community environmental constraints and personal and group relations. The lives of
these women and their involvement in community work are inevitably shaped by sur-
mounting these obstacles and learning from their experiences, both positive and
negative.

Before looking at the community environment and group relations that afflict community workers in their work, two difficulties that community workers also mentioned
are language barriers and time constraints. Some felt that these difficulties were
not as major as other problems. American-born Chinese community workers who did not
speak Chinese expressed frustration at the language barrier, since most community
residents only speak various Chinese dialects. These workers believed that if they
could learn to read and write Chinese, it would eliminate the barrier between them
and not only community members but also the Chinese-born community workers. Even
young activists who took Chinese language courses in their college days expressed
that they still lack sufficient skills to read and write Chinese. Non-Chinese
speaking workers are frustrated because of this handicap.

Three community workers complained about not having enough time. They wished
they had more time for accomplishing projects, meeting deadlines, and getting to know

104

the community better. As one social worker, who works with Chinese adolescents, told me, "I just don't have time and energy and there is so much I want to see done." Time is an important element in doing community work. It determines the amount of effort put into a project, and ultimately, the project's failure. A major problem now looming for many community workers is the period of "hard times," which I will discuss in the following section.

The Community Environment

As a community worker comes to know the community well, she also comes to know its problems. The primary problem is uncertainty generated by changing economic and social conditions in the larger society. Policy changes, cuts in grants and economic recession affect the community. Jobs are always uncertain, especially for a professional staff community worker who relies on grants to fund her job position or her programs in the community organizations. Thus, a professional is always concerned not only about her job but about the impact of cuts on the community programs and the efforts on people who need these services. To outsiders, these changes and instability are not very obvious, but through interviews and close involvement with these women community workers, they revealed to me the pain and struggle of holding jobs with a tenuous future.

One interview struck me as most uncomfortable as I was not aware beforehand that this community worker was experiencing conflict in leaving her job in the community. Lily, who is a teacher at the community school, told me confidentially that her love of working in the community was shattered by changes that affected not only her job but her personal goals. The changes that she referred to were the cuts in funds for the after-school program and the layoffs of a number of teachers in the community school. Smoking her cigarette and looking into space, Lily's faltering voice

105

transmitted the uncertainty she will face when she reaches the end of her term in
working for the community organization. She said:

> I would like to stay...in a community setting, but more
> and more,...I've been thinking, especially in line of
> the cuts from the feds...the community is always reacting
> to all these cuts and we are feeling powerless...we have
> to go wherever so-and-so says, or how the politics is
> played and I'M GETTING VERY TIRED OF THAT.

Workers feel powerless in that they expend a great deal of time and effort in the
community; yet do not have control of circumstances such as funding and budget allocation that are external policy decisions. Moreover, there are fewer job openings
now during these "hard times" as there are less funds being channeled into community
organizations to create and support job positions. The community as a whole is losing staff positions, and programs are being cut. The health center underwent funding cuts on the mental health program for adolescents and the community school received funding cuts on the after-school program. This bad news upset the staff, but
they could do nothing about it. Natalie, a professional community worker that I
interviewed, left for the West Coast and Lily is looking for another job. Community
workers point out that not only the positions were lost but also the skills and expertise, for no one else is able to replace these women who have acquired many years
of experience on the job. Moreover, community workers also lose friends and colleagues, which affects their networking and mutual support.

The political and economic climate of the United States in the 1980's affects
the community in many ways. One of the most important impacts is the limitation on
how much the community workers can do for the community. Jade, a community lawyer,
underlined the conditions that community workers have to face in their work. She
said:

> ...Just a general political atmosphere of this country
> that with all the budget cuts and with the New Rights,
> you know, and all this anti-human services that are
> floating around...create a real difficulty to work in
> the community.

The political and economic situation have diminished the services these community workers can provide. This results in frustration and disappointments that community workers express when they talk about the difficulties of working in the community. There are so many problems and needs in the community and so little funding. Di, a community activist related her feelings of disappointment. She said:

> Well...I get frustrated at certain times. I'm sure everybody does...we can't do much because there are so many problems... [pause and then she said slowly] it's going to be hard.

Ying, also expressed the sentiment that is difficult to cope with the many problems that the community has:

> Not being able to...provide better services for the community ....We are facing cuts...We are always fighting...no, struggling is the word. We're always struggling and that is always a problem.

The "hard times" community organizations are facing is serious. An organization that faces an average 13% cut in grant revenues may lose up to $15,000 or more. Community workers show tremendous concern and anxiety about the future. The alternative is to look into private foundation funding but that requires a different set of fundraising skills that community workers are not familiar with. The realization of hard times and the changing conditions opens a new and unfamiliar realm now that community workers' reliance on federal and state government has been totally shattered. In order for the community to survive, community workers will have to learn new skills and hunt for resources. This requires extra time and effort.

It is through such hard times that the community experiences less factionalization and more cohesion. As Coser (1964:92-95) points out, if an outside threat is perceived to concern the entire group or community, it unites the community and heightens morale. Moreover, it leads to mobilization of energy and increases cohesion as community workers realize that the lack of social solidarity is likely to cause the community to disintegrate. Thus, the community workers that I interviewed tried to see the government policy changes as a positive catalyst towards unity.

107

This positive outlook strengthened the supportive atmosphere community organizations generate. Co-operation and support can be seen in organizations sharing space and programs, and in increased communication about possible directions in obtaining funding elsewhere.

Group Relations

Two areas of difficulty that community workers discussed at length are working with (1) conservative group, CCBA, and (2) working with personality conflicts.

In the midst of all the community organizations that are undergoing changes in services and orientations, the CCBA remains conservative and unchanged. Community workers refer to this foremost organization as the "conservative leadership" in the community, and they talked about experiences of encountering the conservatism of the CCBA.

Dominated by pro-Taiwan, business-oriented members with a traditional view of what the community is, CCBA's purpose remains business-oriented in nature. During a meeting I had with the community school's board, the discussion of CCBA's interest in developing condominiums in Chinatown became a debate on whether to support CCBA. The voting result clearly indicated that CCBA's interest in generating business-oriented activities in the community is not supported by community workers. Community workers also have always opposed CCBA's sole representation in Chinatown. Because CCBA's interests do not coincide with those of community workers, and they do not consult with other organizations, this resulted in a general discontentment and disunity in the community. At the 1970 public hearing and conference which I have mentioned earlier in Chapter 2, the representation issue became public when a community worker pointed out this problem. He said, "Efforts by the young to force social change have been met with 'suspicion and contempt' by elders who wish to maintain a facade of tranquility." He also pointed out, "the older leadership [meaning the

108

CCBA] is still 'Chinese oriented' and American values such as democracy, representation, and freedom have very little place in their decision making."[1]   Efforts of including CCBA by various organizations in solving major problems in the community have failed many times.   For instance, important housing and land issues were ignored by CCBA.   Jade, an activist in the Land and Housing Association, told me of a specific incident that happened two years ago:

> When the issue of job displacement in the garment factories
> ...arose, our organization had gone to the CCBA and invited
> Mr. Chairman to join a coalition that we're working with,
> and we even invited Mr. Chairman to chair the coalition and
> we said that we will be willing to work under his leader-
> ship. Mr. Chairman's response to the group was that CCBA
> is the only legitimate organizations, 'we represent China-
> town and we will not work with other groups.'

When asked what CCBA had done the past two years about this problem, she told me, "I don't want to say they haven't done anything, they only examine the records." She looked at me knowingly for my reaction to her answer.

Organizations that have looked to CCBA for guidance and leadership have come away disappointed and rejected by the insolent attitude that CCBA has taken. A community activist, Emily, who helped Chinese parents form the Chinese Parents' Group told me of an incident that happened to the Chinese Parents' Group and the CCBA. She said:

> ...I went with them to a meeting at Chung-Hwa [CCBA's Chinese
> name], and asked them whether they could help with the busing
> issue. And Chung-Hwa said, 'what do you think we are?' [laugh]
> 'we're not here to do this kind of shit, you know.' So the
> parents were very disappointed. They came back...and told
> everybody. From that experience, they know that they could not
> depend on them [CCBA]. We did everything ourselves. We went
> to the school committees, we went to every single meeting....

Many groups that have approached the CCBA have had similar experiences. They have learned to depend on other organizations within the community for co-operation and support. The role of CCBA in community organizations remains minimal.

Though social organizations have drawn together to cope with community issues and problems, no single organization has emerged to play a leadership role in the

109

community. Community workers and activists regret this lack of leadership. A community resident whom I have known for a long time told me that the lack of leadership is not only difficult for community workers but also community people. She said:

> To tell you the truth, I've been living in this community for
> a long time, I don't even know where CCBA is located. That is
> the same sentiment with a lot of people. CCBA is like a sleep-
> ing dragon, you know: you wake him up once in awhile.

The lack of leadership of CCBA among its own people is sorely missed in dealing with crises, and in the struggle for unity and strength in the community. The support system that the community draws its strength from is weakened by CCBA's disinterest. CCBA is caught up in the preservation of the status quo; unwilling to take a strong stand on issues, and afraid of social changes. Aline, a community worker, made an important observation during a CCBA meeting concerning relocation to a new school being built. Aline recounted CCBA's opposition in the following manner:

> ...the building of the CC school. The intention is, it will
> be a Chinese community center with the Northville Chinese
> Life-Enrichment Committee moving there as well as [CCBA]
> moving inside the center,...and these people [meaning the
> members at the CCBA meeting], they don't want to...Okay, re-
> novations of the CC school is one thing, but if you want the
> CCBA office to move the the CC's School's location, is a big
> NO—NO!! They said, 'This is our office, and this has always
> been our home.'

They held their stand even though they realized that the present office does not provide them with community visibility because it is tucked away in a back corner of a small side street. The move to the new building would provide a central location more accessible to the community, yet the CCBA members opposed such a move.

Women community workers especially, resent the male-dominated CCBA that does not recognize the leading, active roles women play in many social organizations and in the community. Woo, a professional community worker, told me that only recently in 1981 CCBA finally hired its first female administrator. However, there is a lot of mistrust felt among the male conservative group. Woo said, "She's not treated as... inside people...there's a lot of rejection, but fortunately the chairperson is not

110

a very traditional man." Women community workers believe that the female administra-

tor is a token and CCBA has a long way to go in becoming more receptive to women com-

munity workers. One statement about CCBA presented by the community activist, Jade,

is similar to views of other women have about this all-male organization. She said:

> ...they are all men; all the people that sit on the board
> are men....in their by-laws you have to be a male to be
> on the board....

I cut her off and said, "what?" And she continued:

> I'm not sure that's right, but I've heard this from someone.
> I've never seen a woman that sits on the board of the CCBA,
> that's like...over twenty-five years. The president or the
> chairperson has always been a male.

CCBA has a long history of male leaders. In other cities, like New York, women are

not traditionally accepted as CCBA members. Thus, women join other organizations or

form their own to participate in the community (Kwong, 1979).

Community workers who had worked in other cities emphasize that the community en-

vironment in Northville is composed of factions within community groups. Jade, a

community activist who worked for more than ten years in New York Chinatown and

Northville, smiled and looked at me knowingly, and said, "If you can survive working

in this community, you can survive anywhere else." Working in a community that has

a large force that does not welcome other community workers is often a difficult

thing to deal with. Jade recounted her community work experiences in New York China-

town:

> The division among the different groups in Chinatown has
> always been a tremendous obstacle. An obstacle in New York
> and an obstacle here, but I would say that the situation is
> worse here than New York. The reason why I think it's worse
> here is because I don't think that there is a solid base
> community leadership; whereas in New York, there is!! What-
> ever leadership that exists in Northville Chinatown tends
> to be very conservative....I think in New York, people have
> gone away from that. People are more aware that there's a
> need to address issues that concern Chinese Americans and
> not making decision about you as a group; you, as an indi-
> vidual on the basis whether you support Taiwan or China.

Ying pointed out the fact that the Northville's Chinese community has not gone beyond
the conservative issue; whereas in San Francisco community, issues have gone beyond
the point of whether one supports China or Taiwan. She said:

> One...the Asians here are fewer in numbers, I think from the
> statistics you can tell. But over in the West Coast, you have
> about a million. It's people power.
> Secondly, I think that...the East Coast, specifically Northville,
> ...has a much more repressive climate for politics,....there is
> more repression [so] that people don't seem to organize so effec-
> tively to fight the political force.
> The politics here seems the same as...other communities ten or
> fifteen years ago, they all start that way. They all start with
> individual interests and then they move on to broader focuses.
> Community politics: People fighting a lot of time and factions
> ...I think in Northville, you can tell that they're way behind
> because...the conservative forces in Chinatown will assert a lot
> of power in the community.

This is the group environment that every community worker is aware of and has to
deal with. On the other hand, conflict as well as factions, also come from within
the organization. However, one has to realize the importance of conflict as part of
the dynamics of change in the community.

Apart from dealing with the CCBA, the community workers must also deal with personality conflicts. Personality conflicts tend to overshadow and direct community
workers from handling important, immediate goals and issues. Ying expressed this
difficulty:

> I think the biggest problem is finding people who...maintain a
> sense of political principle throughout...work. [Otherwise]
> they get lost because...they fight each other and in competi-
> tion with one another. It's a struggle because sometimes you
> find that you're fighting your own people rather than fighting
> the forces out there and I think we get misguided in our GOAL
> and THAT'S one difficult part about community work.

Since Ying is an activist, she defines community work as political work and community
workers as responsible for maintaining and advocating the interests they share with
other community workers. Racism, inequality, poverty, and sickness are a few of
the social problems faced by the Chinese community. Personality conflicts can result in losing a very good friend and community worker as well as failing to solve

112

community problems and crises. One official community worker resigned because of a personality conflict with the board.[2] The community workers that know her admire her leadership and performance. They told me, "She had a lot of guts," but at the same time admitted that it was very difficult to work with her because of her personality. Her sudden resignation from a community agency a few years ago came as no surprise to those who had worked with her. Cleo recalled that:

> She was very critical of me when I first came in. We haven't talked to each other in years...but I don't bear any grudges ....She was a good community worker and a leader....

Community workers whom I interviewed took this community worker's case as an example of personality conflict that they should avoid. Jean, who knew her, mentioned that her aggressiveness and ambitiousness tended to make her critical and picky. Mao-lin commented about her:

> It was, you know...an obvious move, but,...when I first got this job in the elderly agency and was the first woman to get paid since most of the women at that time participated at the voluntary level, she came and attacked me. The downfall came when she was not supported by the board of directors on her plans...and she has nowhere to turn to.... [shaking her head]

Not being supported by others makes it difficult for a community worker to survive long: a community worker usually ends up resigning. Avoiding conflict is not easy, and as Mao-lin mentioned before, being supported by a board of directors or colleagues is most important in order to be successful in the community work one does.

Community workers come from diverse backgrounds of education and occupational specialties. According to community workers, community work is a learning process, where new skills are learned. Cleo, a past president of the Chinese Life-Enrichment Committee, told me:

> Ten years ago, when I was still sitting at board meetings, ...you have people maybe never done meetings before, and had never sat on a committee. [Today]...at least, most meetings have an agenda...but we are still _training_ people in the community and that's another frustration, it's still a _training_ ground. I think we have to accept that.

113

Due to their lack of experience, community workers find it hard to distinguish between personality and issue conflicts. Examples of issue conflicts are: What per-
cent salary increase should a director get? Are we to support CCBA's plan to build
condominiums in Chinatown? If our goal is in health care, do we have the right to
take up the busing issue? Issue conflicts occur in defining the goal and purposes of
the organization and setting its guidelines. It may appear here that these issues
are technical; however, I have observed discussions where community workers mistakenly
personalized these issues. For example, when the staff is not supportive of the decisions the officials have made, a community worker would exclaim: "I feel betrayed";
"It was not our fault"; or "they are making us feel guilty." Rather than finding a
way to amend the situation, an official may continue to be angry and bring up past
issues that have no relevance to the present discussion. When this happens, one
feels uncomfortable and usually feels it is a waste of time to be there. Heather,
who experienced this type of situation before, told me it happens regularly. She
noted: "It is stupid—this kind of issue. I would never deal with it. It proves
that the community worker has not learned the ropes yet."

Katherine, who helped to build the health center, emphasizes that a community
worker cannot teach others how to handle discussions, but has to allow community
workers to learn through personal experience. Resolving issue conflicts can be
further impeded by the flow of new members to an organization. Katherine comments:

> A community organization should have new people coming in all
> the time....to maintain the life of the community organization.
> But there is a price you pay...you almost always starting at
> zero again.

I asked her why this is so. She replied:

> Every time when a new group comes in,...they have to experience
> the same thing that old people experienced...you can't tell
> people why you don't do this that way because people just have
> to experience this....That's human nature.

Since new community workers are not aware of the status or background of a particular

114

issue, the discussion generally goes back to the beginning to familiarize them. This pattern slows productivity, because it must be repeated for every new worker. As Leonard S. Cottrel (1977:552) points out, "Difficult learning and unlearning is involved in achieving competence in realistic perception of self and other, and in the realistic appraisal of situations."

Conflict is not easily suppressed and avoided. When it exists, it must be recognized and its sources identified. Arbitration, civil procedures and votings are forms of procedures which community organizations have learned to use to bring up the issues separate from the personalities involved.

The community school's board that I observed showed how issues were handled in an efficient manner. As their board meetings average three hours to finish everything on their agenda, the moderator allows two speakers from opposing sides of an issue to express and summarize their points. Ten minutes are alloted to each speaker or representative. Once the issue is discussed, a vote is taken and the result is tabled without further discussion. In staff meetings of the community newspaper that I was asked to join, groups of three are formed to discuss issues. When the groups come together, the discussion is concrete and precise, and points are written down before a vote is called. This is different from board meetings I sat on where everyone will have a say. Discussions became tautological and heated arguments occur. However, every organization proceeds differently to try to avoid wasting time in discussion that may not be relevant to the issue at hand.

Apart from the organization's way of handling conflicts systematically and discouraging personality domination in issue discussions, the community workers also have to learn how to deal with conflict of opinions and interests, and cultivate sensitivity and awareness of colleagues. Jean, a long time community worker explained how she would deal with issues without unnecessary scenes. I first posed the question to her: How do you avoid face-to-face confrontation if there are several

115

points that you do not agree with in a meeting? She answered:

> I deal with conflicts in a very orderly fashion. The finest
> example is: Mr. Ping...when he was recommended for chairman,
> I didn't vote for it...because I didn't feel at that time....
> that he was the appropriate person...he was the only one
> running and I wanted someone else to be running. So, I would
> say, 'I like to make a motion...to recommend so-and-so.'
> I'm being sneaky in a nice way...I want to only get that
> message across, now if somebody picks up on it and see some
> validity to it, great!!! If they don't pick up on it, it's
> their problem....

Here she did not confront the group by standing up and saying, "I don't think Mr.

Ping is the right person." Rather, through her motion, she inferred that she

opposed the recommended person and she had made her stance. Another way of avoiding

personality conflict is to use a tape recorder in meetings. When discussions are

played back it becomes clearer what the issue conflicts are and what the personality

conflicts are. Also, if given time after a heated discussion, people can listen to

the tape in a calm, objective manner, and realize the inappropriateness and pettiness

of personality conflicts. The tape recorder also serves as a checking device. Since

a tape is an official transcript of a meeting, members must make sure their state-

ments are clear, and avoid unfounded accusations or attacks on other members. Jean

finds that writing notes during meetings is helpful:

> I...admit when I bring it up...I always think up what I'll
> say and write down the pros and cons so that I made my
> reasons clear enough.

Burnout

The difficulties and constraints that community workers operate under in the com-

munity environment produces in the long run, stress. One of consequences of the

stress experience by community workers is the serious problem of burnout.

Dr. Freudenberger and Richelson (1981:13) define burnout as "a state of fatigue

or frustration brought about by a devotion to a cause....that failed to produce the expected reward." They say that those who have a sense of mission to fulfill, like the community workers, tend to be the most vulnerable to such a problem. They point out:

> People who choose to go into the relatively low-paying helping professions usually have a sense of mission. They are compassionate and caring, which makes them especially vulnerable to the excessive demands that are made on them (p. 159).

Community workers operate within an environment that creates new needs even as they are trying to meet old needs.

> The population they're dealing with is in extreme need. It is composed of troubled and deprived human beings with a void so huge it is almost impossible to fill it. These people take, drain, demand. They require continual giving and assume an endless supply on the part of the helper (p. 159).

The community worker is sometimes called upon to deal with immediate crises, most of which usually come without warning. Under a time constraint, the community worker is pressured to perform as best as she can. Aline's complaint echoes those of other community workers who are constantly on their feet and who work under constant demands. She said:

> A lot of people...don't understand your difficulty. Any time they want to ask for help, right, they really count on you: 'You have to help me.' If you are unable to help them because of the lack of resources, they don't understand. They just think that you don't want to help them.

This results, sometimes in doing less than what is expected of them, and increases their stress.

On the average, community workers stay at least five years in the community. According to Woo, a professional community worker, usually stays for a long time in the community despite burnout. She, herself, has worked in the community for fifteen years and she observed:

> I think that a person can spend four to five years, and people have to pull back from that because it's very intense...some people have more energy than others, but I think from a person's mental health, a person can only do it for so long, and has to pull back and re-charge.

117

The feeling of burnout is a unique personal experience for community workers. To illustrate how one feels burnout during this stage, Cleo gives the following explanation:

> It wasn't depressive. You just get physically, emotionally, mentally very tired. You have too many people making too many demands on you and you cannot fulfill them all, and you try to fulfill half of that. You probably can't and you're burned out...
> You begin to question your ability. You begin to question your personal roles. Everything becomes personalized and you said...'I can't do it anymore.' That is, to me, burnout.

Ruby, another community worker, said almost the same feeling came to her:

> When you're burnout, it's not even physically. The whole thing is emotionally, you feel that...you're so empty, you're so exhausted. I mean you still enjoy your day-to-day work, but deep down, you know...that you're burned out.

Eventually, they not only question themselves, but also their work. A burned-out community worker, Katherine, telling me that she would not go back to community work, said cynically:

> I just don't want to deal with things at that [community] level. I don't want things to change every two years kind-of-business. I rather work with something that affects public policy; making changes in the system as opposed to making changes on one specific incident. I sort of [have] been sitting back just because of that.

At that time, I did not know that Katherine was burned out. Her strong reaction and cynical way of answering took me by surprise. The day after the interview, I called a friend who had worked with her since they got involved in community work fifteen years ago, she told me that Katherine has been burned out for a long time. I began to understand that her strong reaction was due to the whole burnout process that affects the victim.

Dr. Freudenberger and Richelson point out that the sure signs of burnout syndrome are: tiredness, detachment and cynicism. These same feelings are experienced by women community workers in the burnout process they have in working in the community.

118

Women community workers told me that the first step toward recovery is for-
ulating alternative plans. The most important strategy for one who has a burn-
ut crisis is to take things slowly and to think things over. As Freudenberger
nd Richelson (1981:56) point out:

> It becomes necessary to review our choices and to admit that
> a goal or a career or a relationship was a mistake. People
> who are able to sit down and do this with some degree of ob-
> jectivity open themselves to options and solutions.

After re-evaluating their lives, some workers decide to leave community work.
ome leave permanently, others return to community in a lesser capacity. Both Cleo
nd Lily left community work, but both returned when they found the type of posi-
ions that they wanted and are less-demanding and stressful. Looking back, Cleo
aid:

> I know my life had been richer having...the experience I had.
> I mean, there were many nights when I...have been in tons of
> meetings. I couldn't sit here like this and have a relaxing
> evening, and have dinner with you....That's my trade-off right
> now. I'm at a mature age. It's important to me...to have my
> friends, my social life, but it doesn't mean I'm not doing or
> participating.

Community workers learn to listen to people for warning signs of burnout. Com-
ents like, "Why don't you give yourself a break?" are an important sign that a
ommunity worker needs a rest. Social support is also important, and fortunately
nough community workers turn to the women's network for support and encouragement
hen they feel burned out. Women community workers are very sensitive to such pro-
lems and do not hesitate to give full support to one another. One woman community
orker who uses this type of solution to her burnout crises is Ying. She told me:

> I find different ways of getting support and there's a group
> I can go to...talk about having feelings like that. I have
> friends and people that are very important to me in my life
> and help me make it through.

thers who can afford only short vacations take two or three days off during the
eek, disappearing from the office without telling the staff where they will be

119

relaxing. These women return refreshed and energetic. Those who are able to, take a long leave of absence. Two community workers that I know are taking a year of absence from their jobs and community participation to travel.

It is important that community workers are in touch with their feelings to recognize the exact time when burnout syndrome strikes them. Burnout cannot be avoided by community workers in their demanding work; however, the most important step in facing burnout is to recognize and accept one's limitations in work.

Women community workers, despite difficulties they encounter and disappointments they experience, continue to work in the community. Di, an activist, summed up the resolve that has been strengthened through learning experiences in their involvement with the community. She said:

> I think all of us have changed a lot....we all had gotten
> stronger doing community work. There's a lot of myths
> about women, Chinese women. Community work makes one feel
> that nothing is impossible.

In overcoming difficulties, women have discovered the strength they hold within themselves. Ying pointed out:

> It's not easy...community work requires a strong mind and
> a strong body. A strong mind means you have the energy
> to survive...disappointments, setbacks--politically as
> well as personality--and you really have...the guidance...
> within you to keep you going. We do need that strength
> to fight on...

Community workers have come a long way, and in the difficulties that they encounter and overcome, they acquire more confidence, hope and fulfillment that enriches their lives and the community they work for.

CHAPTER VI   WOMEN OF VALOR

Women community workers are not the stereotypic images that the American public

holds. They are not exotic/erotic, as embodied in the character of Suzie Wong, nei-

ther are they passive/demure.[1] Porno films like "China Lust" and "China Dolls" con-

tinued to be made and shown in the past year in American theaters[2] that totally dis-

torted the character of Chinese women. It is such stereotypes that women community

workers are trying to overcome. Their spirit of fighting for their own rights and

the rights of the community people is expressed in the work they do in the community.

These rights include the right of the Chinese people to survive; the right to be

heard; and the right to prevent direct intervention in policies on housing, educa-

tion, immigration, work, social services and grants.

Disappointments and difficulties co-exist with achievements. In the last chap-

ter, the enduring commitment of the community workers is described. This chapter

looks at their resources of strength: achievements, women's culture, and role mod-

els. Finally, this chapter ends with the women's view of themselves, the role they

play in what they see as the battle of resistance for the Chinatown of today and

tomorrow.

Achievements

One of the main sources that women draw their strength from is their accomplish-

ments. Women confronting difficult situations in the community shared a well-known

Chinese parable about an old man who lived in the North Mountatins in China. His

house faced the south and beyond his doorway stood two mountains, Tai-hang and Wang-

wu, obstructing the way. With great determination, he led his sons to dig these

mountains. His neighbor came by and remarked that it was impossible for the old man

to dig away two mountains. But the old man replied, "When I die, my sons will carry on; when they die, there will be my grandsons; and then their sons and grandsons, and so to infinity. The mountains cannot grow any higher, and with every bit they dig, the mountains will be lower."[3] This parable explains community workers' persistence in their work. Like the old man, they are not easily defeated. Issues, like the mountains, are not impossible obstacles to overcome.

Community workers see their achievements as the main rewards and incentives to maintain their continuance in their community involvement. To them, their work is not measured in terms of how difficult it is, but how important it is to the organization, the community and themselves. Achieving and working continuously become values that they share.

In talking about their achievements, community workers relate that their satisfaction comes from seeing the community grow especially in the area of their interests and goals. Di, an activist with the Chinese-American Experience Organization, said:

> I never thought about personal achievements. I think
> we're getting organized. I feel that's an achieve-
> ment....That's a big achievement.

Ling, an administrator, recounted her moments of achievements, "relocating this program from a barn which was not well-heated...and the increasing of funding." The program she referred to is the adult education school that was set up for workers and immigrants in the community. Like any community-base organization, they started with a small program in a small office building downtown. Not only was it located in the redlight district, it was also poorly heated and run-down. When demand grew for the program and funds were increased, Ling and her co-workers were able to relocate the program to a large modern office in B Street. The school expanded and the program extended to include not only Chinese immigrants but also the Indochinese immigrants in the community.

Mao-lin and Nancy were also glad that the construction of elderly housing in the

ommunity was successful. To them, this is a remarkable accomplishment and a step
orward in dealing with the concerns of the community's elderly. Because the service-
riented organizational model adopted in community work in the early 1970's was so
uccessful, activists were uncertain that their grass-roots approach would meet with
uccess. However, the grass-roots organizations have led to a wider spectrum of serv-
ces that are not only social services related, but are related to other areas in
ulture and recreation. In addition, grass-roots organizations also promote direct
pproach and contact with Chinese community people.

When community workers look back on their years of service, they find it sur-
rising that they have been in the community for such a long time and have achieved
uch results. They maintain a sense of humor about their work and achievements.
nnette, an official who serves the health center's board and is the current presi-
ent, told me, "At least it didn't go bankrupt! And I didn't hire a crook."[4] Since
ommunity organizations are non-profit, at times officials like Annette find it dif-
icult to see how an organization will survive. Organizations tend to be less stable
han private companies mainly because their services are not seen as a product that
an be sold in the market for a profit. Also, because the organization cannot trans-
er losses to the clients, it has to bear the burden of juggling itself out of sudden
rises. All these difficult circumstances make each achievement more valuable.

However, each community worker was quick to point out that she did not take the
ole credit for these achievements. Community work is not individual work; it re-
uires the effort and strength as well as support of others. A common response like
ynn's was often heard:

> It's not only myself...working down there. It is an effort
> that...takes many people. It takes a lot of co-ordination
> and many people working on it together.

arge, an activist who started the Chinese-American Experience, Inc., mentioned that
ounding the organization was not only her achievement but also that of the friends

123

and co-workers who made it possible. She said:

> I wasn't the only one. There were...six of us who did it....
> We spent like half a year doing meetings, and then finally
> one day we decided, hey let's do it! We brought our friends
> over and we asked people to come....We painted the place,
> cleaned it up and that's how we got it, slowly...you do
> things that way, and it's been operating since.

Through the support and friendship of the group, women community workers draw the

determination and optimism that drives them toward their goals.

Women's Culture

In discussing female working style and leadership, community workers distinguish-

ed between themselves and male community workers. I called their unique working

style and leadership qualities, "women's culture," since it is a common behavioral

pattern among women community workers. Ying described this style:

> ...women tend to be...[pause] socialized...to collaborate with
> other people, and always get people's support. Also, we're
> more concerned with other people's feelings, you know, how we
> affect each other. Of course, there are certain women who don't
> give a shit about it, you know, [laugh] co-operating together....

The intimacy that women share in the way they relate to one another is often differ-

ent from the men's. They are sensitive to how they affect one another in their work,

and tend to confer more often with one another in the projects they do together.

Jade, a community activist pointed to the collective spirit among Asian women:

> Most of the Asian women I know who are active in community
> work aren't people that are concerned about roles or author-
> ity. Also the style is much more...[pause] working in a
> collective style and more compromising than men.

The characteristics women tend to have: being articulate, sensitive, co-operative,

and compromising make them unique in their approach to community work.[5]

Women culture, the working style of women is generally accepted by the community

at large. Especially, women community workers who do organizing in the areas of

housing, family, education, health and elderly care are more readily accepted by enants, parents, garment workers, and elderly in the community, whereas in these

ctivities, men rarely are seen knocking on doors because they tend to arouse sus-

icion and fear among residents in a high-crime area. Women community workers that

each out to the community also seem to have more of a personal touch which Su-ling

ecognized in the years of her organizing experience with Chinese community parents.

he said:

> Women that I know are more personal in handling social and
> education issues. Because we share common backgrounds of
> concern, for example our children or the school...we are
> better in reaching out to others. Men tend to adopt a more
> professional attitude that lack a human approach in organ-
> izing parents, tenants. They are less in touch to [sic]
> others, mainly because they never work closely with these
> people and don't really know what to say.

Their common concerns for the community are related and shared easily among women

ommunity workers. Because they share a closeness in the way they work, they also

etter understand each other's difficulties, whether in the work they do, or in their

ersonal lives. It is through this willingness an openness to share that networking

mong women is possible. In describing burnout feelings, women talk about other wo-

en who have been through it, and have encouraged them. In the complexity of their

ork, they know they can call each other about information and strategy. This is a

ommon strength and support, as well as an understanding, that women's culture pro-

ides for the community workers.

Role Models as the Best Strength-Givers

Finally, women's culture also provides role models for women to emulate. Al-

hough role models change as community workers change, many of the community workers

ame friends who may or may not work together with them in Northville Chinatown. But

nowing the role model personally is not important; rather, a woman chooses a role

odel for having certain qualities and characteristics that she admires. Role models

125

give them the incentive and strength they need in doing community work. These role models exhibit the qualities that community workers strive for: dedication, commitment, and concern for people and the community. Moreover, none of these qualities reflect the traditional stereotypes of Chinese women: passive, demure and submissive. Community workers also admire the Chinese women immigrants who work full time in the garment factories, and at the same time have the energy to take care of their family and participate in community meetings and rallies.

Two historical figures serve as role models for many women community workers who have an understanding of China's history. These historical figures have become legendary to Chinese women as examples of courage and willingness to commit and sacrifice oneself for a cause. They also exemplify determination to struggle against negative traditional forms of Chinese values.

One of the historical figure is Mu-lan, an authentic Chinese heroine of centuries ago. Mu-lan took her beloved father's place in the army by disguising herself as a soldier. She fought in battles for twelve years. She is well-admired by men, women and children for the courage, spirit, and endurance she displayed. Lü K'un, a sixteenth century Chinese scholar-official in the Ming Court wrote, "Mu-lan is my teacher."[6]

Another historical figure is mentioned, Ch'iu Chin, a woman who played a part in overthrowing the Manchu Dynasty in the early twentieth century. Community workers with a knowledge of China's revolutionary past hail her as the first leader in China's women's liberation movement. Dr. Sun Yat-san called her, "Feminist Hero."[7] Ch'iu Chin was born in 1875 into a gentry family. Her great-grandfather served as a hsien (province) magistrate. Ch'iu Chin was brought up in a family that placed an emphasis on education. During her youth, she learned how to compose poems, ride horseback, and use a sword. Her marriage at the age of twenty-one did not last long, and she left for Japan eight years later to begin her studies. During her studies in

126

Japan, she became actively involved in the revolutionary movement and came back a year later to do political work. She was head of the revolutionary party in Tsua-chiang, and started the first feminist magazine, Women's Journal (Nu-pao). She was arrested together with her comrades in an unsuccessful revolt in Anhwei. The plan was prematurely launched. When she was told the news that the plan had failed, she did not run and hide; and was arrested. Under severe torture, she refused to confess the names of her other comrades, and was beheaded on July 15, 1907, at the age of thirty-two.[8]

Her spirit, devotion to duty, courage, and self-sacrifice inspired subsequent women revolutionaries. Women's armies invoked her spirit during the 1911 revolution.[9] Apart from her political deeds, her essays and poems are read by many. The late Chou En-lai praised her works and considered her one of the best contemporary writers.[10] Heroism means great sacrifice. Women must go through difficult passage of breaking away from family bonds and defying authoritarian traditions. Ch'iu Chin serves as a role model for these women. When she left her husband, she committed an act that was never done at that time. She left her children and friends and the security of life in China to strike out and begin a new life of study in Japan. Kuo Mo-jo, a Chinese writer, praised her as the incarnation of Ibsen's Nora.[11]

An interesting point about these two women heroines is that their role is a masculine one--they know martial skills, they wear men's clothing,[12] and fight in battles. The most important difference is that they do not conform to the standards set for women to behave or live by, and they struggle and fight for others, and for their country. Likewise, Chinese women community workers fight for the rights of other Chinese people, and for the Chinese community. It is because of this particular goal and purpose that they remain in community work, and see that their struggle is crucial in fighting for the Chinese people in a colonized community.

Community work is vital to the community especially in worsening economic times, when minorities need services, support and political organizing more than ever. By grass-roots organizing and participation, community workers hope to help the community residents assert their right to survive as a community. Community workers recognize that the people must ultimately be the force to push for the rights in controlling their own lives in the community. The battles that are fought on the colonizers' ground are difficult for one who has to learn the rules of colonizers and the established system. Armed with this accumulated knowledge, one is then in the system to defend the collective interests. This is the new tradition of women community workers in their struggle for a united Chinese community and to better the lives of the Chinese-Americans.

CHAPTER VII   CONCLUSIONS: SUMMARY AND IMPLICATIONS

This study is about the involvement of Chinese women in the community. It is written to demonstrate and clearly dispel two major misconceptions of the Chinese-American communities in the United States and the role Chinese women play in these communities. Firstly, a Chinese-American community is not a docile, apolitical and isolated cultural entity. It is not a passive community that subjects itself to institutional racism and oppression without fighting back. Community work is a necessary form of organized resistance toward negative external forces. It also offers services and support to not only meet the immediate needs of the Chinese community but also to strengthen the people to assume a better community of tomorrow.

Secondly, women's roles are no longer centered within the boundaries of familial and kin relations only. For the past forty years, their ties have widened and their visibility as active participants of the community has grown, as they have assumed important positions alongside the men in shaping the forces in the Chinese community. Women in the community are active pioneers and vanguards of community activism. The myth of Chinese women as passive and demure must, once and for all, be dismissed by the reality of the position Chinese women hold in society today.

This chapter summarizes the important functions and contributions of Chinese-American women community workers; and the implications for future research within the Chinese-American community context.

The Struggle between Now and Then

Community work is related to the needs, problems, and political activism of the community. Through the construction of community work in three stages: pioneering, professional and activist; the emergent political nature of the Chinese community can be clearly understood. Community work is a necessary ingredient of a community

129

based polity to deal with community crises, from the civil war in pre-1949 China and the invasion of outside institutions into the community, to day-to-day issues and problems. Women's involvement in the community is not merely a vague desire "to do something useful"[1] but a response to the real situation of Chinese people, both within and outside of the community.

Second, community workers perform different levels of various functions that are necessary to the community. Their degree of commitment and dedication determines the importance community work will hold in their lives; structuring their outlook, capability, consciousness, time schedule, and availability. The construction of the subtypes of community workers: volunteers, professionals, officials and activists, allows us to understand how their backgrounds lead them to involvement in the Chinese community. Moreover, the subtypes also are useful in looking at the pattern of community involvement at a specific point in women's life. Table 2 below summarizes the life of community workers at which community work begins for them:

Table 2 The Life Patterns of Community Workers

Types	Life Patterns of Community Workers
Volunteer	COLLEGE------→HOUSEWIFE●------→(with children) (student)
Professional	COLLEGE------→WORK IN COMMUNITY
Official	●COLLEGE------→FULL TIME JOB/COMMUNITY INVOLVEMENT
Activist	●COLLEGE------→WORK IN COMMUNITY/COMMUNITY INVOLVEMENT

● starting point of involvement

The community workers that I sampled conform to these patterns. However, there are some exceptions, for instance, student volunteers, whether they become activists or not, may also start early in their community work career. Since both officials and

activists start early in doing community work before or during college, the differ-
entiation is made that activists are oriented towards outright participation in the
grass-roots politics of the community and interact with community people more often
than officials do. Activists are the new generation of community workers emerging
to shape future community organizations' structures. They are anti-professional
and anti-service and are setting a pattern of participation that is relevant to community structure for the years to come.

Third, the strategy of community work centers and depends on the organizational
personal network system within and outside the community. This system goes beyond
the familial kinship levels on which traditional Chinese organizations are structur-
ed. Women's contacts are wider now. Their ties extended toward the government and
private corporations, universities, national associations, and foundations as well
as friends. An influential and successful network system is multipurpose: to create
a useful and effective bank of information and resources; to give support; to recruit
potential community workers; and to organize and mobilize forces inside and outside
the community for action regarding the Chinese and Asian population. A contemporary
network system is a strategy and a tool in reaching and uniting as well as consolidating ties among Chinese and other Americans that may not necessarily be community-
bound.

Fourth, community work is not a high-paying job. The workers accepts its constraints and enjoy the enriching experiences. The difficulties lie within a community environment that has the policies of a larger society imposed on it; these policies and regulatory control affect the community as well as intra-group relations.
Working under such conditions produces various types of stress. The most common
hazard is burnout. Even when women experience burnout symptoms, many search for
alternatives that will enable them to continue their community participation in a
less stressful way. Women community workers do not give up easily, and are admired

131

by all with whom they come in contact: co-workers, friends, community residents, parents and students.

Community workers dispel the myth of Chinese women as quiet, passive, reserved and docile. On the contrary, they are outspoken, active and courageous. They build their strength and support, and their ability and confidence around the network system and group work. Community work is not individual work, but the combined strength of community co-workers whom they admire. Their success and achievements are on one level, personal, yet on another level, the achievements of the community.

The women use role models for direction in their work. These role models, whether fellow workers or historical figures, all have certain qualities that community workers admire. Women role models hold a unique position, in that they are vanguards in social change, whether they live in China or in the United States. These women, like community workers, are struggling and fighting for the community and for the Chinese people. Community workers also find themselves in a unique position. By believing in themselves and their abilities, and taking action; they are vanguards in creating a better tomorrow for their community.

The Struggle for a Better Tomorrow

The concern I have for the community where I did my study shaped the following questions of its future: What will become of the Chinese community, especially Northville Chinatown? Will community organizations turn toward private individuals and private foundations/corporations for further survival in their funding resources? Will grass-roots level participation be adopted by other service-oriented organizations? Will community activist organizations combine with service agencies in the future? What forms of community work and what types of community worker will serve as the future resistance? I ponder these questions constantly as I am leaving both

132

the community and the work I have grown attached to. The community's history is like an unfolding story with interesting plots but without an ending.

Clearly, the community organization has come to an important juncture. It can no longer depend on government funding for its services and programs. The Reaganomics era has had important consequences and impact. Service organizations are re-examining their goals and purposes as well as their strategies and resources.

Also, the community is no longer a homogeneous entity. The composition of the immigrant population has diversified, due especially to the recent influx of the Indochinese immigrants into the community. This has created additional needs of the Asian population that the community must deal with. Community workers are constantly aware that they have reached a turning point, where new resources, services and segments of the Chinese and Indochinese population groups are going to change the total picture of the community. Community work must adopt and incorporate these changes.

The future of grass-roots level participation seems promising. The present warming relationship between the United States and People's Republic of China has prompted community activists to be in the forefront of expressing their cultural roots through organizing trips to the People's Republic of China and giving cultural performances that were once banned or unpublicized during the CCBA pro-Taiwan era.

On the other hand, community activists, whose radical politics were formed during the anti-Vietnam war period in the mid-1970's are more concerned with the larger issues at hand, such as racism, equality, oppression, violence and war, identity and stereotypical images. Their activist experiences in college were carried forward to their community work in Chinatown. They are more visible because they take active resistance in the forms of demonstration, rallies, and boycotts in order to be heard and seen by society at large. Clearly, we will see more visible forms of resistance in the future.

While this study centers around the women community workers in the Chinese

133

community, this study is only a preliminary step towards understanding the historical development of community work and women's activism in the Chinese community. It is fragmented in terms of background on the long and rich history of Chinese women that still lies dormant behind the memories and images of yesterday. Particularly, the history of the pioneer women that constructed the very first community organizations of New York (Kwong, 1979) and Northville. These women are getting old, and most of their different strategies and survival techniques are important and to be recorded and fully examined.

Although the internal colonial model provides a perspective in looking at the impact and structure of oppression as well as in looking at the separatism movements, cultural nationalism and liberation struggles as forms of political action, the role of women and their resistance experiences need to be incorporated into these studies; for they also live under the rules of colonialism.

This study provides implication in two particular areas. First, it is important to recognize that the network system in the community is a valuable source of and means to resistance that is used among community workers. It is necessary to examine fully the ties that are not community-bound, class-bound and ethnically-bound, but cut across these boundaries. This study describes how women extend their networking ties, but the knowledge on this particular area is rich, and should be further researched, particularly the process of different types of networking, their strength and intensity, an in-depth view of their specific purpose of usages, and the extensions to the government system, academic circles, corporate and private industries, national unions and associations. Related to the network system is the process of recruitment. Particularly, the recruitment of potential members for participation in the community and the mobilization of different segments of people should be fully studied.

Second, the women's resistance movement under colonialism is often seen from the familial perspective as exemplified in the studies of Mina Davis Caulfield (1972, 1974), and Carol B. Stack (1974), but women have moved beyond the familial bounda- ries into the public sphere of the community and the working environment. It is crucial to examine women in the different settings. The study of women's community work provides a public realm that is examined here. Moreover, it provides an impli- cation that forms of resistance and maintenance in shaping the community at large can be seen from different points. For instance, women's grass-roots participation is another area of research that is opened to how women reached out to the community and organize themselves. Issue-oriented research is another way of examining impacts and strategies formed by women to combat crises and problems. This study provides only education and housing as issue examples, but areas that are equally important, such as health, marital conflict, tenants, unions, media, crime and safety, and so- cial class issues, need to be further examined. To recognize such active resistance on the part of the Chinese-Americans is crucial to the consciousness of the common sources of oppression that are faced by Chinese-Americans today.

APPENDIXES

APPENDIX A   SAMPLE BACKGROUND AND CHARACTERISTICS

VOLUNTEERS	Organization	Place of Birth	Education Completed	Marital Status	Age	Occupation
Ann	Dragon Boat/GNCA Chinese Parents Assoc.	Taiwan	Undergrad.	Married	30s	Housewife
Ming	HLA/Chinese-American Experience Org.	Venezuela	+Postgrad. (law)	Single	20s	Student
Ruby	GNCA	Hong Kong	+Postgrad (media comm.)	Single	30s	Student/Housewife
Heather	Northville Foundations, Inc.	U.S.A.	Postgrad (education)	Married	40s	State Govt. Employee
Jane	GNCA	Taiwan	Undergrad.	Married	40s	Housewife
Ma-fan	Eastern Asian American Students Assoc./Chinese-American Experience Org.	U.S.A.	+Undergrad.	Single	20s	Student
Natalie	Chinese-American Experience Org.	U.S.A.	Undergrad.	Single	20s	Museum Employee
Cecilia	GNCA/Chinese-American Experience Org.	Taiwan	Doctorate (linguistic)	Married	40s	Housewife

GNCA = Greater Northville Chinese Association (suburban)
Chinese American Experience Org. = Chinese-American Experience Organization

+ to be completed and still in progress

APPENDIX A (continued)

PROFESSIONALS	Organization	Place of Birth	Education Completed	Marital Status	Age	Occupation
Ling	Adult Education School	U.S.A.	Undergrad.	Single	30s	Administrative
Woo	CCBA	U.S.A.	Undergrad.	Married	30s	Administrative
Angie	Chinatown Health Center	Hong Kong	Postgrad. (Social Work)	Single	30s	Staff
Aline	CCBA	Hong Kong	Undergrad.	Single	20s	Administrative
Nancy	Chinatown Elderly Center	U.S.A.	Undergrad.	Married	50s	Administrative
Mao-lin	Chinatown Elderly Center	U.S.A.	Undergrad.	Single	50s	Administrative
*Lily	Chinatown Community School	U.S.A.	Undergrad.	Single	20s	Staff
Lucille	Chinatown Community School	Hong Kong	Undergrad.	Divorced	30s	Administrative
Nettie	NCLEC	U.S.A.	Postgrad.	Married	20s	Staff

* also official

140

APPENDIX A (continued)

OFFICIALS	Organization	Place of Birth	Education Completed	Marital Status	Age	Occupation
Millie	Chinatown Health Center/Adult Education School	Hong Kong	Postgrad. (Bus. Admin.)	Single	30s	Financial Analyst
Cleo	NCLEC/Dragon Boat	U.S.A.	Undergrad.	Single	30s	Corporate Public Relations Rep.
Katherine	Chinatown Health Center	U.S.A.	Postgrad. (Law)	Married	40s	Federal Govt. Employee
Mimi	Chinatown Nursing Home	U.S.A.	Postgrad. (Social Work)	Married	50s	Private Hospital Social Worker
Annette	Chinatown Health Center	U.S.A	Postgrad. (M.D.)	Single	30s	Medical Doctor
Jean	Chinatown Economic Affairs Organization	U.S.A	Doctorate (Education)	Single	30s	Owner of private consultancy firm
Geraldine	Chinatown Health Center	U.S.A.	Postgrad. (Law)	Married	30s	Lawyer
Lily	Chinatown Health Center	U.S.A.	Undergrad.	Single	20s	Staff (teaching)

141

APPENDIX A (continued)

ACTIVISTS	Organization	Place of Birth	Education Completed	Marital Status	Age	Occupation
*Jade	HLA/Chinatown Health Center	Hong Kong	Postgrad. (Law)	Single	30s	Lawyer
Candice	Chinese Progressive Inc.	U.S.A.	Undergrad.	Married	30s	Teacher
*Lynn	Chinatown Community School	Hong Kong	Undergrad.	Married	20s	Legal Assistant
*Ying	Chinatown Community School	U.S.A.	+Doctorate (Psychology)	Single	30s	Psychologist
Emily	Chinese Progressive Inc./Chinese Teachers Assoc./Chinese Parents Assoc.	U.S.A.	Undergrad.	Married	30s	Teacher
Di	Chinese Progressive Inc./Chinese-American Organization	U.S.A.	Undergrad.	Married	30s	Temporary Postal Worker (laid-off)
Su-ling	Chinese Parents Assoc.	Hong Kong	Undergrad.	Married	30s	Teacher
San-san	Chinese Teachers Assoc./Chinese Parents Assoc.	U.S.A.	+Postgrad.	Married	30s	Teacher

* also official
+ to be completed

APPENDIX B   TYPES OF ORGANIZATIONS

Traditional

Chinese Consolidated Benevolent Association (CCBA)
      An umbrella agency that includes family associations. Pro-Taiwan. For more de-
      tail, refer to Chapter II, "The Emergence of Community Work," and footnotes.
      The office is located in a side street, Ox Street in Northville.

Northville Chinese Women's Club
      Members are older generations of women who also belong to family associations.
      The club started in the 1940's. For more detail, refer to Chapter II, "The
      Emergence of Community Work." I call these women, "Pioneers/Volunteers."
      Office is located in Ox Street. I had visited and interviewed two members
      (in their 70s and 80s) from this organization with the help of a Toisanese-
      Cantonese translator.

Service

Northville Chinese Life-Enrichment Committee (NCLEC)
      The very first social agency that opened in Northville Chinatown. The social
      services include providing information about housing, immigration, education,
      and job placement and referral. Also provides classes in language, referral
      services to other social agencies and translation work. The Dragon Boat office
      and staff are located also in this center. It is situated in Ox Street.

Chinatown Community School
      Community school in Northville that has a twenty-year history. The school is
      located in Wayne Street in Chinatown. There are five programs in this school:
      After-school Program, Day-care Program, Day-care Center and Regular School, with
      English as a Second Language (if needs arise), Recreation Program (for students
      and adults), and Adult Education Program.

Adult Education School
      A special vocational school for new immigrants and workers in the community.
      It not only provides language proficiency but also holds vocation skills and
      job training. Joint program with Chinatown Economic Affairs Organization.
      Office is located in B Street.

Chinatown Health Center
      A clinic that provides health services to the Chinese population in Northville.
      It celebrated its tenth anniversary in 1982. The office is located in the
      community school building in Wayne Street.

Chinatown Elderly Center
      Provides some health-related services, but mostly recreational activities and
      learning experiences for the senior citizens. Some users come from suburbs of
      Northville for the center's activities. They also provide transportation serv-
      ices for the elderly. Its Hot Lunch Program is well admired in the community.
      For the past ten years, the center has provided hot lunch for the elderly for

only .50 cents per person. The office is located on the first and second floor of an elderly housing project in Wayne Street.

Other service organizations

There is also a Youth Association that provides social services for Chinese teenagers. Because of its policy of not giving interviews to researchers and students, I was unable to contact anyone in this agency that was willing to provide me with more information. There is also a YMCA in Northville Chinatown that provides recreational services for the youth and adults in the community.

Activist (Grass-roots)

Chinese Progressive, Incorporated

The organization is located in B Street. A pamphlet that I picked up during a conference in the Chinatown Community School provides the following information about the organization: "CPI is an organization for the people of Chinatown and the Chinese community. Our three principles are uniting Chinese people to improve their welfare and lives, support of all progressive people, and support for the People's Republic of China." The center provides translation services, recreational activities for workers, youth, retired people, and shopkeepers. Currently they have about 120 full-time members in the organization taking part in issues like housing, tenants' right, workers' rights, and education development (in bi-lingual program).

Chinese-American Experience Organization

A small organization next to the Chinese Progressive, Incorporated. Members work on Chinese-American history projects, music performances and providing classes for Chinese and Western musical instruments, and dance. Recently they also started an oral history project of obtaining valuable information about Chinese-American history in Northville.

Chinese Parents Association, Chinese Tenants Association, and Chinese Teachers Association

These associations are grass-roots participation associations for Chinese people in the community. Meeting places are fairly mobile, in homes or the offices of Chinese Progressive, Incorporated.

Housing and Land Association (HLA)

Another grass-roots organization that deals with tenants' rights, and complaints as well as working with garment workers and community organizations that are displaced by land encroachment in the Chinatown area. They also provide legal consulting services. This particular service are joint with the Greater Northville Legal Services that cater to the communities in the Northville area.

Eastern Asian-American Students Association

This activist organization is not community based. It is a national association based in a Eastern college. Members are involved with the community, particularly one project that this organization has is an annual "college day" event held in the community. They provide information for admission to the colleges around the Northville area. The student members also are affiliated with the Asian-American Experience Organization in Chinatown and provide joint performances and programs for the Chinese population in the Northville Chinatown area.

144

Asian Women Organization
    This activist organization is a women's network group. It is not community
    based. Majority of the members work in the community. They provide work-
    shop projects like poem-writing and reading, women's consciousness-raising
    sessions. Meetings are held once a month in members' homes.

Suburban

Greater Northville Chinese Association (GNCA)
    An organization that provide films, cultural projects, resettlement services
    for Indochinese refugees, and educational projects for the Chinese suburban
    children and adults. Most members are from professional, middle-class back-
    ground. Meetings are held in suburban homes for its members. Most members
    are also linked with Chinatown's official and professional community workers
    and community organizations such as the Land and Housing Association, health
    and school boards, the Chinese Parents Association and the Chinese Teachers
    Association.

145

APPENDIX C   ON THE METHODS USED IN THIS STUDY

This section is a detailed account of the research I conducted in Northville Chinatown. The subject of Chinese-American community workers and their involvement in the community has never been treated. Thus, this study is exploratory and is a beginning attempt at identifying and understanding the relationships that exist rather than predicting them. The inductive procedure that this exploratory study takes to discover significant variables and basic relations enables my research to encompass the multifaceted levels and divisions of community work and is not confined by a hypothetical deductive model (Katz, 1953:75). This particular approach is useful in providing not only a vivid picture of the role women community workers play in the community, but also the problems and crises Northville Chinatown faces in the American society. The concern for the community is not only felt by those who live there but also by those who work there.

The Background and the Beginning of Research

My contact with Chinese women community workers started three years ago when I was studying the professional role of American-born Chinese women. In the course of my research I found that nearly half of the women I interviewed participated actively in community organizations. This was an area of work in addition to, and often but not always separate from, the nine-to-five jobs they held in the labor force. These women not only had a tighter time schedule but also more responsibilities than ordinary working women. Compared to women who did not participate in the community, this group of community workers seemed to have a wider and more cohesive social network. Their community work also enhanced their self-esteem and made them advocates of community participation as an intrinsic value.

These Chinese professional women who were community workers provided me with rich narratives about their lives that highlighted the community context. While there was rivalry among colleagues, there was also strong mutual admiration for the changes endured and problems that these community workers overcame while working for their respective community organizations. The depth of these experiences inspired me to go beyond my previous research[1] on their work in and for the Chinese community and the critical role women play in the community setting.

The Entry

Since I am an outsider to Northville Chinatown, I did not rely on interview data alone. First, I examined secondary resources to get to know the Chinese community better and second, I explored various ways of gaining access to the community through participant observation. The secondary resources that helped me in my preliminary fieldwork included a research report done by the redevelopment authority in Northville; copies of the community newspaper, Dragon Boat, put out by a social service agency called Northville Chinese Life-Enrichment Committee; pamphlets and reports produced by organizations that I visited; information conveyed at conferences that I attended and conversations with community workers that I knew. These materials sensitized me not only to past events that shaped community life but also to the present situation in the Chinese community. This detailed and multifaceted approach was essential to the study of the community workers in their work setting. Participant observation enabled me to experience first-hand the forces affecting the organizations. I was able to comprehend the situation and hence my personal involvement led to a far better understanding of the difficulties and problems faced by

---

1. See my unpublished M.A. Thesis, "Chinese American Women and their Working Lives: An Exploratory Study," Boston University, 1979.

147

community workers than I could have obtained merely from interviews. The two organizations that I became involved in provided me with experiences and skills that are
useful in the community setting and I have come to appreciate them just as other community workers in my study have learned in the process of their work.

My present research began a year before my research writing in 1982 when I first
contacted the Northville Chinese Life-Enrichment Committee Center where the past
issues of community newspapers starting with 1972 were kept.[2] The staff there was
helpful in providing me with the necessary community documents and a conference report that the agency has kept for references. In the course of two months, I finished reading every issues of the newspapers. At the same time, I also looked at clip-
pings from the Northville's major newspaper, North Star, about events that happened
in Chinatown. The North Star's articles were on general events, but those of the
Dragon Boat covered more events, and were more detailed. Most useful were the edi-
torials in Dragon Boat that covered subjects ranging from bi-lingual education to
immigration policy changes. When I finished reading, I asked again for any newspapers that covered Chinatown during the period preceding the 1970's, but, according
to community workers there and the women I came to interview later, no such records
were kept. At the present, community activists are aware of such an information gap
and have begun to plan for a new oral study project,[3] but it will not be completed
until 1984.

---

2. The community newspaper, Dragon Boat, is put out by the Northville's Chinese
    Life-Enrichment Committee. It first started out as the Committee's newsletter
    to its members in 1972 and later became the only community newspaper in North-
    ville Chinatown. The newspaper is in Chinese and English, and is published
    monthly.

3. The community activist at Chinese Progressive, Incorporated began the project
    in August 1982. The goal, according to the project co-ordinator, is to "capture
    some of the daily life struggles of the oldtimers", see the August issue of
    Dragon Boat (1982) for more detail.

In collecting materials for the study, I took careful notes of important past events; of the community leaders; and of the various developments of agencies around the neighborhood and their problems. This background provided me with an important source of reference, was helpful in formulating my proposal for the present study, and also served as a preparation for my later stage of involvement with the community in Northville.

During the time spent in the Northville Chinese Life-Enrichment Committee Center, I observed the community workers (who are the paid staff) working with everyday people who walked into the office in search of housing, immigration guidelines, translation work, college and job information as well as courses offered by the Center. This beginning stage of observation was important to me because I realized then that relying exclusively on interviews and questionnaires is a very limited way of understanding the community workers. Here, I saw them at work. I was sometimes mistaken for one of the staff, and because of my ability to speak and understand Chinese I made an effort to be helpful whenever I was approached in that office. I made friends with the staff who are mostly young, college-educated and bi-lingual. Even though their qualifications may easily get them jobs outside the community, these workers have opted to stay and are fully dedicated to serving the community as their vocation. Their expertise at providing information about housing, education and vocational training programs, immigration procedures, and language translation is valued by the people who desperately need their help; particularly those who are new to the community and Northville itself. Some clients who had been helped came back to say hello and stayed to chat with the staff. While I was there, I listened to their conversation with the staff workers and I realized that these clients feel that they have friends here whenever they need information or help in solving troubles in their personal lives.

My entry into community involvement in Northville Chinatown began when a good friend, active in the community and knowing that I was trying to begin my study, suggested that I should apply to become a board member in a health agency. This friend was one of the contacts I had maintained since my previous study was completed three years ago. I realized that my participation on the board would allow me to go inside an organization to see community workers at work from a different level of participation that I had observed before and in addition, it would give me a broader perspective by being a community worker myself. So, a month after her suggestion and help I was nominated to sit and participate on the board, and thus began my own initiation into community work in Northville Chinatown. I learned while looking back upon my earlier participation that social networks within the community are an important element of community, for a year later my nomination to a second organization's board was also dependent on another friend and community worker's help.

From my own participation, I realized what community workers mean by knowing people, by "touching base." In the world of community work, community workers cannot work alone. The relationships among community workers at different levels have to be maintained constantly and the bonds between community workers in Northville help them not only to support each other but also to facilitate the actions that the community has to take in dealing with community issues. The social network (Hunter, 1953) is the conduct through which forces are channeled for the survival and unity of the community.

The Sample and Interviews[4]

The primary source of data in my study came from open-ended interviews with

---

4. The interviews were in English and Chinese. I translated the Chinese portion for this study. Some interviewees spoke English as a second language and therefore, were not always grammatically correct. I left their comments intact and did not edit them.

150

thirty-two women community workers.[5] Criteria that I used in selecting the community

workers were: (1) they must be active in community organizations. By the word "ac-

tive" I mean that they participate at least six hours or more per month in meetings

and organizational activities; (2) they must have been working two or more years for

the community organization(s). This allows them to speak from a rich experience and

familiarity with community issues and community work when they spell out the result

they see from the process of change and development in the community; (3) they are

recommended by community workers and highly regarded as "contributors" to the commu-

nity. By that I mean women community workers who have received awards, or are men-

tioned in the community press, or those who have contributed and are known to be

active in areas such as bi-lingual education, busing, housing, health and immigra-

tion and are seen as an asset to the organization itself.

I did not use criteria such as age, or place of birth because such specifications

would disqualify certain community workers who are active and working in the communi-

ty. Moreover, community workers who know each other, without exception, do not use

such criteria to look at each other's work and performance, or as a reference to dis-

criminate against another from participating in the community. Community workers

that work in the community see and learn from each other's experiences and perform-

ances regardless of whether that person is in her 20's or 60's, or whether she is

born and educated in Asia or in the United States.

"Snowball" sampling was used to accumulate an initial list of community workers

because it proved to be impossible to locate subjects by random procedure as there

were no complete lists of potential subjects.

Based on preliminary fieldwork I identified four subtypes of community workers:

---

5. Although I only included thirty-two women in formal detail in my study, my
    findings include other formal and informal interviews I had with other women
    community workers I encountered during my own participation in the community.

volunteers, professionals, officials and activists This allowed me to contact women in different levels of positions in the community. I also made known to them my ob-servation of subtypes of women community workers after the interview was over and asked for comments. Thus, they were able to give me a complete list of women they had come to know as volunteers, professionals, board officials and activists. Since the active community workers who devote so much of their time to the community are both well-known and well-recommended, it was easy to gather names. The community is fair-ly small and women community workers know each other well. The emphasis on the list they each provided also gave me a sense of different networks to which they belonged.

I started my interview five months after my initial entry into the community work was underway. This period of time allowed me to know more community workers well and I maintained a good relationship with these workers so that later I could talk and discuss my project with them and obtain names and further advice. Numerous male colleagues on the board who knew me well also discussed my project privately with me and confirmed my thesis that women community workers have always undertook leadership roles in Northville Chinatown. They named the women leaders and the roles they play in each of their organizations and I came away with the names of at least two women who played an important role in most social agencies in Northville Chinatown. It was clear at this point that women are recognized as the active ones in the community. In the two organizations that I was involved in, I found that women are often more outspoken and decisive than the men and they took leadership roles on the boards and committees in their respective organization.

The names and information on my list were of community workers who were mentioned repeatedly.[6] As I am aware of sampling bias in research, I never stopped trying to

6. The background information of these four types of community workers: occupation, age, marital status, education, place of birth, organizations they belonged to, are in Appendix A.

interview all on the list that was given me by a community worker, neither did I start interviewing the women right away. It is clear to me that a sampling bias occurs when a network, an organization or a category is over-sampled. Community workers themselves never gave me a long list of names but cautiously picked the ones that they knew best. Moreover, they did not give out names easily unless they knew what I was looking for. By categorizing my community workers into four subtypes, it helped them to indicate clearly who they had in mind and the importance of their selection. In addition, I also made known to them if I had interviewed the person they have named so that I did not have duplicates. It is always good to go over the list with the community workers during the interview so that one knows the detail and the reasons for their selection.

I made a total of forty contacts and came away with thirty-two participants for my study.[7] In addition to the forty contacts I made, I also conducted informative interviews with men colleagues, past community workers that had long retired and friends who were working in various organizations in the community. Over 80% of my sample were women community workers in Northville Chinatown that I had either conducted intensive or informative interviews and discussion with. During the last part of my fieldwork interviews women community workers had trouble giving me more new names. Either I had interviewed them all or I knew them personally and had talked to them about my project. I finally sat down and used another approach with the

---

7. In the forty contacts that I made, five refused to be interviewed as explained in the following paragraph in this section. Three women I interviewed gave me very short and general answers that I found difficult to include in my study. Even though they were willing to be interviewed in the beginning when I called them on the phone, the interviews revealed a certain degree of reluctance to talk openly with me. Of the three women interviewed, two have left community work, and the last woman was on the verge of leaving, but I did not know this until the 1982 nomination was over. By then I had finished collecting all my data from the thirty-two women that I wanted.

153

help of a community worker and friend. We listed all the agencies in Chinatown and then looked through my list to find how many women community workers in each organization I had interviewed or had not yet contacted. During our intensive discussion, I found that I had interviewed at least two, but not more than four, women community workers in an agency. I realized then I had a fairly well-distributed sample. My friend suggested however, that I interview two suburban Chinese-American organizations The suggestion was well-taken and these women were included in the formal thirty-two women sample.

I kept a log of all the calls I made and of the conversations. The telephone log became the first preliminary data indicating just how busy these thirty-two women really were. When the women that I wanted to interview were not in, I made sure that I called them again because they kept long and unpredictable schedules and could never return my calls, even when I left a message. Three women set up appointments to see me (at least three weeks ahead of time) but had to postpone them because of crises that came up. Two women postponed and rescheduled three appointments that were canceled one after another. It was about four to six weeks before I could sit down with them. Most of the women asked me to call back because at the moment they were occupied. It was a long and tedious task doing interviews and appointments with these women and it was fortunate that I was not working or going to school during this time.

Five women refused to be interviewed. Two women who were officials had gone through a long and painful period during their community work and felt because of personal reasons that they did not feel comfortable sitting down and talking about their work in the community. Two other community workers who were professionals were in the middle of proposal deadlines and important projects, and were reluctant to spend their precious time away from their work. One professional refused to be interviewed by a student, fearing that more students will come to her and her time will be taken elsewhere. Even though I felt very upset when potential participants refused to be interviewed, I never used my community reference or involvement to ask for favors. The main reason was that I was not doing a study for the organizations and I had not obtained consent in using the organizations' names. I felt that identifying myself as a student and giving my purpose for doing the study was the first thing I should get across to the potential participant; and then when I established a rapport with my participant my own experiences as a community worker could be a conversation topic that I could mention during my interview.

During the period of interviewing, I learned that there are numerous things that should be taken into consideration as a researcher. One is that it is easy to feel discouraged and dejected when community workers asked me to call back or refused to be interviewed because of their busy and unpredictable schedules. One has to keep on trying and pursuing the potential participants. This persistency of the researcher always pays off in the end. It is also important during this period to keep track of the time spent on setting appointments. I gave myself a two-week deadline to contact the community workers who said that they were too busy to see me the first time. Thus, I had a guideline to follow to avoid wasting too much time to obtain an interview. I found that the participants were busy with their own priorities and commitments and would often not return calls. In the end, it is the researcher that has to press to set up a time as soon as possible for an interview.

The second thing about interviewing is that it is important that the participants know who you are and your personal background, in addition to the exact project that you are doing. One has to build trust at the initial contact with the potential participant and let her know that her participation is important to the research study. If the participant wants to know about the interview schedule, it is crucial that the researcher does not avoid giving out necessary information. I never terminated a telephone conversation, and additional conversation always generated interesting

155

discussions which were equally important to the study, even though the interview schedule did not cover that. I have come to realize that telephoning is an essential contact and networking tool to be used, and that community workers have always made time for this kind of discussion within and out of their community work.

The third and last important consideration about interviewing is the role of a student. I have come to know that when one mentioned that one is a student, the participant either take an interest in you or your project or wants to avoid you right away. Community workers especially do not hold a good impression of students. Most community workers had worked with students before and found that many students were not "sincere." Sincerity to them, means full commitment and good intentions in doing community work. However, students (some of them) because of their school assignments could not devote themselves full-time to community work. Other students also have used their participation merely as a reference to put on their resumé and this is something that community workers frowned upon. Moreover, releasing names and information without permission from organizations and community workers had created embarassment in the past and further clouded the image of students. This particular issue had caused a lot of suspicion and distrust among the community workers that I have known.

As a student and researcher, stepping into this troubled water is not easy. The researcher could avoid associating with these suspicious community workers. However, considering the research that one must undertake, it is essential that one should not cause a wider gap for I knew that agencies have closed their door because they could not deal with students of this sort. During my interviewing, I realized how important it is to seek advice from community workers on how one can take the steps to prevent this kind of problem. It is important to me that although my fieldwork is completed, I never use this as a reason to break away from community involvement and friendships. One has to maintain the ties that were established and it is a

156

responsibility that a student should bear in mind whenever acting as a participant and a researcher in the community setting.

I spent four months interviewing community workers. Two of the interviews were conducted in my home because the community workers were close friends of mine. Thirteen of the interviews were conducted in the homes of the participants. Many hours were spent on the road going to places outside of the Northville area. At times I became lost, so determined to find my way I made sure that I started traveling early. The interviews that were conducted in the evenings at the participants' homes took longer to complete. The informal atmosphere and sometimes good food generated many interesting discussions. The rest of the women asked me to come to their offices. Because of the busy schedules these women kept, the interviews were interrupted at times by phone calls and visits from colleagues. However, these interruptions were sometimes very important because I could see how women work within a tight schedule. It is very interesting that these women have very good memories: they remembered things that happened long ago and yet minute things did not escape their attention. They were very alert and on the phone I could see that they dealt with crises very well. For example, when a colleague called up about a crisis meeting, a worker would be on top with the latest plan and know exactly with whom this colleague ought to talk to before the crisis meeting was held. Or if someone called to talk about a budget problem, they would provide information, both primarily and peripherally related off the top of their heads. These were split-second decisions: names and telephone numbers or an exact deadline were given without fumbling around in a notebook to check for accuracy. Interviews that were conducted in the office were long and sometimes exhausting and I made sure that I had ample time to spend with them and had no immediate appointments to rush to. I spent an average of three to five hours with each community worker who talked about her work and her personal experiences.

However, there were also interviews that ran only two hours long and proved just as valuable to my research.

A focused interview schedule was used. First, I tested the schedule with two community workers and they offered very useful advice and directions that were adopted later in my submitted proposal. The response I got from my focused interview schedule was good. Many participants said that it brought them so many memories, both sad and happy, that happened in the past; it also made them aware of turning points in their lives. A few thanked me because the interview schedule came at a period when they were examining their own goals, aspirations, and achievements. The interview schedule helped them to formulate new directions to where they wanted to go in their lives. For them, the interview schedule was an occasion where they could reflect and think about themselves in their world of community work. An opportunity to sit back and talk about what they did and are doing was very rare.

The interview schedule is essentially divided into four parts: Description of participant's life and community participation, their perspective on the community and its problems, the view of community work and workers in the community organizations, experience in doing community work and finally their socio-demographic backgrounds. Topics are first mentioned by the interviewer and the participant responds and elaborates until a particular topic is fully covered.

Twenty-seven interviews were taped, however, not all the conversation was taped. Sometimes, the participant requested that I turn off the tape because certain information that they gave was very sensitive. I never objected to these requests. I felt it is considerate for the researcher to do so at certain points when the participant becomes personal or feels uneasy. Five other interviews in my study were not taped. Two of the private offices did not have outlets for my tape recorder and going elsewhere would deprive them of privacy. Others refused to be taped because they did not feel comfortable with a machine. Some interviews were filled

158

with Chinese phrases (either Cantonese or Mandarin) because the participants felt that they could better express themselves that way. For example, the proverb that is used frequently by those who speak Chinese: The sky is high, the Emperor is far. This is taken to mean that no one is going to know about what she or he is up to when the authority is away, or one has more flexibility and freedom. Some words, for example, "Yi Wu" could not be translated simply to an English word. The meaning is a combination of "obligation, duty, dedication and commitment." A bi-lingual community worker who works with the Chinese section of the community newspaper, Dragon Boat, told me that one loses much in the meaning that one wants to convey when translating a language, and the essence disappeared through the translating process. Phrases in Chinese are written down in Chinese characters in my transcripts because I recognize that the true format of the Chinese language conveys their philosophy, principles and ideals that are shared by those who use the Chinese language. Until translation became necessary later in my writing, I kept the conversation in Chinese in their original form in my transcript.

The Analysis

The taped interviews were transcribed immediately together with other important fieldnotes I took during the interview. Immediate transcribing was necessary so that I could retrieve important materials from a fresh memory retained after the encounter with the community workers; any missing points would be followed up by contacting the person again. Included in the data were fieldnotes about the places that I had visited whether it was a house or the office of the individual participants that I interviewed. These transcripts were easy to read and provided first-hand materials that were important in understanding the role women play in the community. The tapes that were transcribed were stored away for references. In addition, I also wrote down my own interpretations, opinions, ideas, and experiences in a field diary. I

159

called it a diary instead of a journal because it also included my personal emotions, and biases that I encountered in my fieldwork. As my research progressed, reading and re-reading my diary was very useful in providing guidelines and information to fall back on.

As my fieldwork came to an end, I started to organize my data into specific themes and topics of importance, such as the topic of "conflict and factions," where I describe the types of conflicts and factions, who the participants are that encounter them (for example, participant #0219, page number of the transcripts), and the development of conflicts (page number of the transcripts of participant #0211). Under the topic of "burn out" I outlined the number of burn-out cases I interviewed, how many recovered or are still recuperating, the symptoms of burnout (refer to transcripts #2111 and #3122, #0214); change of career that occurred (refer to transcript #0214, #0180), and how many activists versus officials encounter burnout. I did likewise for topics under "gender," "organizational role," "social networks," "community problems," "community events" and "community work history". These topics are like the index section of a book where one can refer specifically to the participant's transcripts and the page number as well as my field diary and notes on my files. These systematic indexes which highlight the different themes of women's community work proved useful in helping me to organize and develop my writing of the chapters.

As I created and organized topics and themes of topics from my data, the picture of their life history began to take shape: how they began doing community work, and the process of their work that influenced their own growth and development. I developed useful charts and graphs. For instance, in looking at their intensity of participation, I developed the following time span chart. (See Figure 1 on next page)

From the chart, I can see that community workers have been involved in community work for quite some time. The officials, for instance, have an average of thirteen years of experience in community work; activists also participated for an average of

160

eleven years in the community. The professionals and volunteers spend an average of eight and nine years in the community as the community organizations only started ten years ago. Charts such as these are very useful and exciting, for one can see the patterns forming in place from the bulk of data that I have gathered.

Figure 4   Intensity of Participation by Types of Community Workers

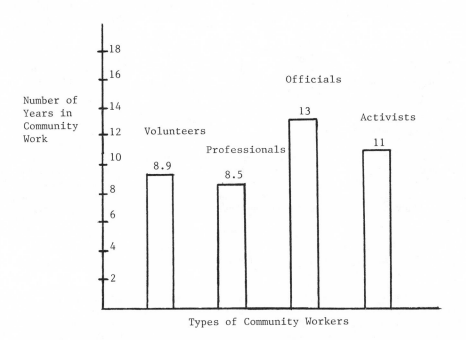

From these data, I produced a short summary report of findings and this short summary helped me to formulate a workplan for the chapters I wanted to write and the topics of readings that I wanted to complete on my own. Moreover, it became clear from the data analysis, that community work was not just a nine-to-five job for these women but part of the history of Northville from the past to the present and the struggles of Chinese Americans in the community.

161

Introduction

1. For more details on Chinese-American studies and their orientation, see Lucie Cheng Hirata, "The Chinese American in Sociology," in Counterpoint: Perspectives on Asian American, ed. Emma Gee (Los Angeles: University of California, 1976), pp. 20-26.

2. Source: U.S. Department of Commerce, Bureau of the Census, Subject Reports: Japanese, Chinese and Filipinos in the United States, PC(2)-1G, 1973, Tables 7, 22 and 37; and U.S. Summary 1970's, Table 224. Also, from United States Commission on Civil Rights, Success of Asian Americans. Fact or Fiction? (Clearinghouse Publication 64, September 1980).

3. The names of individuals, organizations and the research site have all been changed to protect their privacy.

4. Hirata (1976) mentions that some unpublished works have been done recently. In her footnote she reveals the following works: Isao Fujimoto, "The Legacy of Internal Colonialism and Its Impact on Asians in America," and John Liu, "The Internal Colonial Model and the Asian American." (p. 26). However, I was unable to find these works for this study because her original sources did not reveal where these working papers are presented.

5. For more in-depth study on the historical exclusion and ordinances, refer to Stanford Lyman, Chinese Americans, Chapter Four on Anti-Chinese Movement in America, 1785-1910 (New York: Random House, 1974).

6. Senator Allen Simpson, chair of the subcommittee on immigration is attempting to eliminate the Fifth Preference, or remodel the Fifth Preference so that the definition of close family should conform with American ideals and values rather than from other cultures. For more detail, refer to Dragon Boat, January/February 1982, p. 7.

7. See Chapter 1 in this study.

Chapter I

1. To protect my participants' privacy, more detailed historical data of Northville Chinatown could not be provided.

2. From a report put out by the Planning and Evaluation Department of the Action for Northville Community Development (ANCD), The Chinese in Northville, 1970 (Northville, 1971).

3. From the ANCD 1971 report, p. 19.

4. For more detail of the immigrant laws and its effect on Chinese, see Stanford Lyman, Chinese Americans (New York: Random House, 1974), the chapter on Institution Racism.

5. According to the 1980 census, there are 297,462 females as opposed to 265,326 males.

6. The 1980 census data in this study is provided by the information services specialist in the census library in Northville. Data was released in late 1981.

7. The 1980 census, like any other census data on minority communities, tends to underestimate. The Chinese ethnic group is suspicious of outsiders gathering these kind of statistics, so the figures provided in this research are lower figures, which many Chinatown organizations' administrators use even though they are aware of the undercounts. To get this particular figure and others, census track calculation is necessary. The Northville Chinatown consists of three census tracks that are totaled to make this particular figure and other figures that are presented in the study.

8. Also from ANCD report in 1971.

9. From the Administrative assistant in CCBA.

10. From the 1981 report put out by the Economic Development Corporation of Northville (EDIN).

11. This is an interview translated from a Chinese newspaper, Get Together, March 1982. The series are a set of interviews about immigrants' lives in the United States.

12. I attempted to find the juvenile delinquency rate of Chinese immigrants in Northville Chinatown. No agency, including a youth center whose social workers are assigned to help kids in trouble had such delinquent reports. I then checked with the police records, but it was not broken down into ethnic groups. All authorities, including the police detective friends that I met during my translator's work at the Superior Court, could not help and they cautioned me that any records or delinquency rates that I get tend to be an undercount. In my final desperation, I went to the library. The American Statistic Index, based on FBI reports, provided some statistics on delinquents arrested; however, it is not broken down into cities, and had only a national delinquency rate figure. Of the total crimes that are committed by Chinese, the 1979 and 1980 reports state that 11% (1979) and 13% (1980) were committed by juveniles. It is not valid to conclude that Northville Chinatown has a high delinquency rate based on such a report. Chinatown has to be properly surveyed in the future if delinquency of juveniles is to be studied.
To understand more of the problems caused by the recent generation of Chinese kids, refer to Kaoru O. Kendis and Randall J. Kendis, "The Street Boy Identity: An Alternative Strategy of Boston's Chinese Americans," Urban Anthropology, 5, 1(1976): 1-17. This article relates the importance of peer groups in the everyday life of community children when their parents need to work and they are left alone at times to fend for themselves.

13. For more detail, see the chapter on the elderly in Asian Americans: An Agenda for Action. A conference summary put out by the New York State Advisory Committee to the United States Commission on Civil Rights (Washington, D.C., 1980).

14. I relied very much on the theoretical literature of underdevelopment and dependency in the understanding of the internal colonial situation of the third-world minority communities in this country. Both Lyman (1974) and Blauner (1972) recognized the internal colonization of third-world communities and its development, but do not examine the internal workings of each minority community's situation in detail and also do not fully examine the interdependent relationships that are going on at the present time. For my study, I relied on Fernando Henrique Cardoso's and Enzo Faletto's work, Dependency and Development in Latin America (Trans. Marjory M. Urquidi, Berkeley: University of California Press, 1979) for an understanding of the colonial and neo-colonial enclave economy.

Chapter II

1. For more detail about the types of Chinese traditional organizations, see Stanford Lyman, Chinese Americans (New York: Random House, 1974). The chapter on the Chinese Community Organizations in the United States.

2. The eleven organizations represented on the board of the Chinese Consolidated Benevolent Association are: The Chinese Businessmen's Association; The Northville Chinese Life-Enrichment Committee; the Nationalist Party; the Freemason; the Northville Chinese Community Church; the YMCA; the Northville Chinese Women's Club; the Lun Association; a seamen's group; the Hung Soon Association; a business club; the American Legion Post; and a Chinese Music Club.

3. The Chinese Consolidated Benevolent Association (CCBA) in the United States is pro the Republic of China (Taiwan). Many of its members were members of the Kuo Ming Tung. Conflict arose when other community organizations expressed sentiments for the People's Republic of China. The normalization of relations between the People's Republic of China and the United States was a blow to the CCBA, because it weakens the support for the Taiwanese government. Community workers in the community told me that if one is advocating for change in the community, this person will be labeled a "communist" or a traitor. The progressive element which is the Pro-People's Republic group in the community received a lot of hostility when it first got started in Northville Chinatown, although Pro-People's Rebpulic organizations established in American Chinatowns are not a recent phenomenon. For more detail, see Peter Kwong, Chinatown, New York (New York: Monthly Review Press, 1979).

4. My research only concerns organizations that contribute directly to the community. There are Chinese women who contributed to outside organizations which are not taken into account in this study.

5. Refer to Peter Kwong, Chinatown, New York, pp. 99-100 on the Chinese Women's Patriotic Association (New York: Monthly Review Press, 1979).

6. Source from a report published by the Northville Chinese Life-Enrichment Committee, "The Future of Chinatown." (March 1972).

7. "Progressive Movement" is a term used commonly by community workers and activists. It is not to be confused with the 1960's progressive era and the progressivism during this period. It is used here to refer to organizations developed in Chinatown to advocate for the issues of Chinese people, such as workers' compensation, workers' rights and unionization. These issues are seen as progressive because they advance

164

the position of Chinese people who are workers in the United States. The organizations that are developed are people-oriented rather than business-oriented. In New
York and San Francisco, the progressive organizations developed during the 1930's.
For more detail, refer to Peter Kwong, Chinatown, New York (New York: Monthly Review
Press, 1979). For example, the Chinese Worker's Mutual Aid Association is also a
progressive organization because it addresses the rights of workers and the right to
aids that Chinese people should get. The Progressive Movement that is people and
grass-roots oriented is not a recent phenomenon.

Chapter III

1. This community worker was formally a volunteer and has also worked with the
city's community service agency where she was assigned to Chinatown. She has been
involved for five years; however, this particular administrative position is new
and she had just started a year ago.

2. For more detail about the burnout crisis community workers suffer in their work,
see Chapter Five.

Chapter V

1. From the North Star,   "Chinatown Charts Future," October 25, 1971.

2. This woman community worker whom I interviewed for my M.A. study (1979) was a
capable, energetic individual. She was fired, according to one source, but may have
resigned. Because of her forthright personality and outspokeness, she encountered
conflict with board members; and being a director for an agency, without full support, her work became difficult. I have heard that she remains inactive and has
not taken any outside career since she resigned. A close friend of hers, Ruby,
told me they never mention the past when they talk; and moreover, after she left
the Chinese community, Ruby felt that they never would be close again.

Chapter VI

1. Juanita Tamayo Lott and Canta Pian, "Beyond Stereotypes and Statistics: Emergence of Asian and Pacific American Women," (Washington, D.C.: Organization of
Pan Asian American Women, 1979).

2. Source: Dragon Boat, "Porno Films Exploit Chinese Women," (May 1981), Northville.

3. Also told by the late Chairman Mao Tse-Tung, see Ruth Sidel, Women and Child
Care in China (Baltimore, Maryland: Penguin Books, 1973).

4. Officials on the board make major decisions also on recruitment of personnel
in their community organizations.

5. A common observation that community workers made about men's working style is that men are more concerned about their professional and authoritative roles. They also choose to sit on committees that bring them high visibility with outside agencies. Men's working style is also discussed at length in a study done by Ronald Lawson and Stephen E. Barton (1980) on the tenants movement in New York City.

6. From Lü K'un's work, Kuei Fan (Po-ju chai tsiang pan ed., ca. 1613). Also quoted in Joanna Handlin, "Lü K'un's New Audience: The Influence of Women's Literacy on Sixteenth-Century Thought," p. 23 in Margery Wolf and Roxane Witke (eds.), Women in Chinese Society (Stanford: Stanford University Press, 1975).

7. "Tsin Kuo Ying Shiong" 巾帼英雄. "Tsin Kuo" means the "feminist' or "women," and "Ying Shiong" means "hero" and in the Chinese language, "Ying Shiong" is a neutral noun. See the epilogue of Ch'iu Chin Tze Liao 秋瑾史料 (Historical Biographies of Ch'iu Chin), ed. by Chao S.S. et al. (Hunan, China, 1981).

8. The story of her life and work is also written in English by Mary Backus Rankin, "The Emergence of Women at the End of Ch'ing: The Case of Ch'iu Chin," pp. 13-66 in Margery Wolf and Roxane Witke (eds.), Women in Chinese Society (Stanford: Stanford University Press, 1975). Her biographies in Chinese were compiled in Ch'iu Chin Tze Liao (Historical Biographies of Ch'iu Chin), ed. by Chao S.S. et al. (Hunan, China, 1981).

9. See Ch'en Tung-Yaan, Chung-Kuo Fun-nu Sheng-hua Shih (History of the Chinese Women),(Shanghai, China, 1928).

10. See the epilogue of Ch'iu Chin Tze Liao (Historical biographies of Ch'iu Chin), ed. by Chao S.S. et al (Hunan, 1981).

11. Kuo Mo-jo, Mo-jo Wen-chi (Collected Writings of Kuo Mo-jo), (Peking, China, 1959), p. 12.

12. In Japan, Ch'iu Chin was always seen in men's clothes. Photos have been taken of her posing in Chinese men's attire. Pictures are found in Chao S.S. et al (eds.), Ch'iu Chin Tze Liao (Historical Biographies of Ch'iu Chin), (Hunan, 1981).

Chapter VII

1. Doris B. Gold, "Women and Voluntarism," in Woman in Sexist Society, eds. Vivian Gornick and Barbara K. Moran (New York: Mentor Books, 1972), pp. 533-54.

SELECTED BIBLIOGRAPHY

American Statistics Index
   1979   Juvenile Delinquency. Annual and retrospective edition. Washington,
             D.C.: Congressional Information Services.

   1980   Juvenile Delinquency. Annual and retrospective edition. Washington,
             D.C.: Congressional Information Services.

Blauner, Robert
   1972   Racial Oppression in America. New York: Harper and Row, Publishers, Inc.

Blauner, Robert and David Wellman
   1973   Toward the Decolonization of Social Research. In The Death of White So-
             ciology. Joyce A. Ladner, ed. New York: Vintage Books.

Bonacich, Edna
   1979   The Past, Present and Future of Split Market Theory. In Research in
             Race and Ethnic Relations. Cora B. Marrett and Cheryl Leggon, eds.
             Greenwich, Connecticut: JAI Press Inc.

Bott, Elizabeth
   1957   Family and Social Netowrk. London: Tavistock Publications.

Cardoso, Fernando H. and Enzo Faletto
   1979   Dependency and Development in Latin America (Trans. Marjory M. Urquidi).
             Berkeley: University of California Press.

Caulfield, Mina Davis
   1972   Culture and Imperialism: Proposing a New Dialectic. In Reinventing
             Anthropology. Dell Hymes, ed. New York: Pantheon.

   1974   Imperialism, the Family, and Cultures of Resistance. Socialist Revolu-
             tion 30, Vol. 4, No. 2:67-85.

Chao, S. S. et al. (eds.)
   1981   Ch'iu Chin Tze Lia (Historical Biographies of Ch'iu Chin). Hunan,
             China: Hunan Publishing Company.

Ch'en, Tung-yuan
   1928   Chung-kuo Fun-nu Sheng-hua Shih (History of the Chinese Women). Shanghai.

Coser, Lewis
   1964   The Functions of Social Conflict. New York: The Free Press.

Craven, Paul and Barry Wellman
    1974   The Network City. In The Community: Approaches and Applications. Marcia
            P. Effrat, ed. New York: The Free Press.

Dong, Lorraine and Marlon K. Hom
    1980   Chinatown Chinese: The San Francisco Dialect. Amerasia Journal, 2 No. 1
            (Spring):1-29.

Fainstein, Norman T. and Susan S. Fainstein
    1974   Urban Political Movements. Englewood Cliffs, New Jersey: Prentice-Hall,
            Inc.

Freudenberger, Herbert J. and G. Richelson
    1981   Burn-out. The High Cost of High Achievement. New York: Doubleday and
            Co., Inc.

Gans, Herbert
    1962   The Urban Villagers. New York: The Free Press.

Garcia, John A.
    1977   Community, Autonomy, Advocacy, and Representation: A Latino Community
            Organizational Model. In New Perspectives on American Community. Roland
            L. Warren, ed. Chicago: Rand McNally Publishing Company.

Gold, Davis B.
    1972   Women and Voluntarism. In Woman in Sexist Society. Vivian Gornick and
            Barbara K. Moran, eds. New York: Mentor Books.

Granovetter, Mark
    1973   The Strength of Weak Ties. American Journal of Sociology 78 (May):1360-
            80.

Handlin, Joanna
    1975   Lu K'un's New Audience: The Influence of Women's Literacy on Sixteenth-
            century Thought. In Women in Chinese Society. Margery Wolf and Roxane
            Witke, eds. Stanford: Stanford University Press.

Hayner, N. S.
    1930   Social Factors in Oriental Crime. American Journal of Sociology 43 (May):
            908-11.

Hirata, Lucie Cheng
    1976   The Chinese American in Sociology. In Counterpoint: Perspective on
            Asian American. Emma Gee, ed. Los Angeles: Asian American Studies
            Center, University of California.

Hirsch, Herbert
    1973   Political Scientists and other Camaradas: Academic Myth Making and
            Racial Stereotypes. In Chicanos and Native Americans. Rudolph O. de la
            Garza, Z. Anthony Kruszwski and Tomas A. Arcinego, eds. Englewood Cliffs,
            New Jersey: Prentice-Hall, Inc.

Hsu, Francis K.
    1974   The Challenge of the American Dream: The Chinese in the United States.
            Belmont, California: Wadsworth Publishing Company.

Huang, Tsen-ming
    1954   The Legal Status of the Chinese Abroad. Taipei: China Cultural Service.

Hunter, Floyd
    1953   Community Power Structure. Chapel Hill, North Carolina: North Carolina
            Press.

Jacobs, Paul, Pual Landau and Eve Pell
    1971   To Serve The Devil. Volume 2: Colonials and Sojourners. New York:
            Holt, Rinehart and Winston.

Jacobson David
    1975   Fair-weather Friend: Label and Context in Middleclass 'Friendships'.
            Journal of Anthropology Research, Vol. 31:225-236.

Kalish, Richard A. and Sharon Moriwaki
    1973   The World of the Elderly Asian American. Journal of Social Issues 29,
            No. 2:187-209.

Kanter, Rosabeth Moss
    1977   Communes and Commitment. In New Perspective on the American Community.
            Roland L. Warren, ed. Chicago: Rand McNally College Publising Company.

Katz, D.
    1953   Field Studies. In Research Methods in the Behavioral Sciences. D. Katz and
            L. Festinger, eds. New York: Holt, Rinehart and Winston.

Kendis, Kaoru Oquiri and Randall Jay Kendis
    1976   The Street Boy Identity: An Alternative Strategy of Boston's Chinese
            Americans. Urban Anthropology 5, No. 1:1-17.

Kroeber, Theodora
    1970   Alfred Kroeber: A Personal Configuration. Berkeley: University of Cali-
            fornia Press.

Kuo, Chia-ling
    1977   Social and Political Change in New York's Chinatown. New York: Praeger.

Kuo, Mo-jo
    1959   Mo-jo Wen-chi (Collected Writings of Kuo Mo-jo). Peking.

Kwong, Peter
    1979   Chinatown, New York: Labor and Politics, 1930-1950. New York: Monthly
            Review Press.

Lawson, Ronald and Stephen E. Barton
    1980   Sex Roles in Social Movement: A Case Study of the Tenant Movement in
            New York City. SIGNS: Journal of Women in Culture and Society, Vol. 6
            No. 2 (Winter):230-47.

Lee, Rose Hum
    1956   The Chinese Abroad. Phylon 17, No. 3 (Autumn):257-70.

169

Lewis, Helen, Sue Kobak and Linda Johnson
    1973   Family, Religion and Colonialism in Central Appalachia or Bury My Rifle
            at Big Stone Gap. In Growin' Up Country. Jim Axelrod, ed. Clintwood,
            Virginia: Council of the Southern Mountains.

Li, Peter S.
    1977   Occupational Achievement and Kinship Assistance Among Chinese Immigrants
            in Chicago. The Sociologist Quaterly 18 (Autumn):478-89.

Light, Ivan
    1973   Ethnic Enterprise in America. Berkeley: University of California Press.

Light, Ivan and Charles C. Wong
    1975   Protest or Work: Dilemmas of the Tourist Industry in American Chinatowns.
            American Journal of Sociology 80, No. 6 (May):1342-68.

Lofland, Lyn H.
    1975   The 'Thereness' of Women: A Selective Review of Urban Sociology. In
            Another Voice. Marcia Millman and Rosabeth Moss Kanter, eds. New York:
            Anchor Books.

Lott, Juanita Tamayo and Canta Pian
    1979   Beyond Stereotypes and Statistics: Emergence of Asian and Pacific American
            Women. Washington, D.C.: Organization of Pan Asian American Women.

Lu, K'un
    1613   Kuei Fan. China: Po-ju Chai Tsiang Pan. (ca. 1613).

Lyman, Stanford
    1974   Chinese Americans. New York: Random House.

Mayer, Adrian C.
    1966   The Significance of Quasi-Groups in the Study of Complex Societies. In
            The Social Anthropology of Complex Societies. M. Banton, ed. American
            Sociological Association Monographs, 4. London: Tavistock Publications.

Milgram, Stanley
    1969   The Concept and Use of Social Networks: In Social Networks in Urban
            Situation. J. Clyde Mitchell, ed. Manchester, England: University of
            Manchester.

Nathan, Richard P. and Paul R. Dommel
    1977   The Cities. In Setting National Priorities: The 1979 Budget. Joseph
            A. Pechman, ed. Washington, D.C.

Nee, Victor and Brett de Bary Nee
    1973   Longtime Californ': A Documentary Study of an American Chinatown. Boston:
            Houghton Mifflin Company.

New York State Advisory Committee
    1980   Asian Americans: An Agenda for Action. A Conference Summary. New York.

Payton-Miyasaki, Yuriko
    1975   Three Steps Behind and Three Steps Ahead. Asian American Journal. Los
            Angeles: Asian American Studies Center, University of California Press.

Rankin, Mary Backus
    1975   The Emergence of Women at the End of the Ch'ing: The Case of Ch'iu Chin.
            In Women in Chinese Society. Margery Wolf and Roxane Witke, eds. Stan-
            ford: Stanford University Press.

Schwartz, Howard and Jerry Jacobs
    1979   Qualitative Sociology. A Method to the Madness. New Yor: The Free Press.

Sidel, Ruth
    1973   Women and Child Care in China. Baltimore, Maryland: Penguin Books.

Siu, Paul
    1953   The Chinese Laundryman: A Study of Social Isolation. Unpublished Ph.D.
            Dissertation. University of Chicago.

Stack, Carol B.
    1974   All Our Kin. Strategies for Survival in a Black Community. New York:
            Harper Colophon Books.

Stonequist, Everett V.
    1937   The Marginal Man. New York: Charles Scribner's Sons.

Sung, Betty Lee
    1971   The Story of the Chinese in America. New York: Collier Books.

    1976   Survey of Chinese American Manpower and Employment. New York: Praeger
            Publishers.

U. S. Bureau of Census
    1973   U. S. Summary, 1970's. Washington, D.C.

    1973   Subject Reports: Japanese, Chinese and Filipinos in the United States,
            1970. Washington, D.C.

    1980   Census of Population and Housing, Northville. Washington, D.C.

U. S. Commission on Civil Rights
    1980   Success on Asian Americans. Fact or Fiction? Washington, D.C.: Clear-
            inghouse Publication 64.

Thompson, Richard H.
    1979   Ethnicity vs. Class: An Analysis of Conflict in a Northern American
            Chinese Community. Ethnicity 6:306-26.

Valentine, Bettylou
    1978   Hustling and Other Hard Work. Life Styles in the Ghetto. New York: The
            Free Press.

171

Wang, Paul
    1972   The Emergence of the Asian-American Movement. Bridge 2, No. 2:33-39.

Wax, Rosalie
    1971   Doing Fieldwork. Warnings and Advice. Chicago: The University of Chicago
            Press.

Weiss, Medford S.
    1974   Valley City: A Chinese Community in America. Cambridge, Massachusetts:
            Schenkman Publishing Company.

White House Conference on Aging, 1971
    1972   Asian American Elderly. Washington, D.C.: U.S. Government Printing Office

Whyte, William F.
    1955   Street Corner Society. Chicago: The University of Chicago Press.

Wirth, Louis
    1958   Urbanism as a Way of Life. American Journal of Sociology 44 (July):3-24.

Wu, Cheng-tu
    1972   Chink! New York: World Press.

Yap, Stacey G.H.
    1979   Chinese American Women and their Working Lives: An Exploratory Study.
            Unpulished M.A. Thesis. Boston University.

Zinn, Maxine Baca
    1979   Field Research in Minority Communities: Political, Ethical and Methodo-
            logical Observation by an Insider. Social Problems 27, No. 2:209-19.

Materials on Northville

Action for Northville Community Development (ANCD). The Chinese in Northville,
    1970. Northville: Northville Redevelopment Authority, 1971.

Economic Development Corporation of Northville Report, 1981.

Dragon Boat, October 1980; May 1981; October 1981; January/February 1982; August
    1982.

Get Together, March 1982

Northville Chinese Life-Enrichment Committee (NCLEC). The Future of Chinatown.
    Northville, 1972.

North Star, October 25, 1971.

Chinese Progressive, Inc. What is CPI?   April 1981.

INDEX

Ace University; 13, 32-33, 37-38, 78, 102

Action for Northville Community Development; cited 12, 22

Adult Education School; 143

Anti-Vietnam Movement; 75, 77

Asian-American Elderly, The; cited 20

Asian-American Experience Organization; 144

Asian-American Movement; 2, 36, 75, 77-81 83

Asian-American Women's Group; 80-81

Asian Women Organization; 145

Blauner, Robert; cited 3, 24

Boston Italian community; destruction of 13-14

Bott, Elizabeth; cited 95

Burnout; 116-120, 131; recovery from 119-120

Catholic Church; 28

Caulfield, Mina; cited 3, 6

Children; 17, 19-20, 28, 88

Chinatown Community School; 143

Chinatown Economic Affairs Organization; 143

Chinatown Elderly Center; 143-144

Chinatown Health Center; 143

Chinese-American Experience Organization; 37, 144

Chinese Consolidated Benevolent Association; 3-4, 27-28, 143, 164; conflicts 108-112

Chinese Parent's Association; 37-38, 109, 144-145

Chinese Progressive, Incorporated; 37, 39, 76, 144, 148

Chinese Teachers Association; 144-145

Chinese Tenants Association; 144

Ch'iu Chin; 126-127, 166

Civil Rights Movement; 75

Colonialism; whites over Chinese 3-6, 22-24, 134; Chinese resistance to 6-7, 24, 75, 128-129, 133-135

Community work; 6-7, 104, 121; activists 75-83, 85, 130-131, 160-161; conflicts 83, 101-102, 108-116; cooperation 97, 107-108, development of 25-26, 28-41, 83, 129-130, frustrations 105-108, 131; goals 78, 84, 127-129; involvement 43-85, 130; linkages 86-103, 131, 150; motivations for 50, 52-54, 58, 60-63, 66, 68-74, 80-82, 100-101, 104, 116-117, 120-124, 127-128, 146; as necessity 24, 32, 37-38, 43; officials 64-74, 85, 130-131, 160-161; political support of PRC 30, 144; professionals 55-64, 83-85, 105-106, 117, 130, 161; recruitment 99, 165; sexual differences 124-125, 152, 166; stresses 116-120; training 114-115; volunteers 45-54, 66, 73, 84-85, 130, 161

Cottrel, Leonard S.; cited 115

Daycare; 16, 143

Divorce; 17-18

Dragon Boat; 48-49, 94, 143, 148

Economy; 23

Education; 39, 79; adult 122, 143; bilingual 47-48, 144; changes in 77-78, 100; Chinese Teachers Association 144; busing 37-38, 79, 100, 109

Elderly; 20-21, 143-144

Employment, Chinese; 4, 15-16, 20, 88; benefits v, 16; unions 4, 16, 79, 164; of women 2, 16-18, 56, 64-65

Ethnic bifurcation, Chinese; dialect 14-15; political 101-102, 108-109; sexual 124-125, 152, 166

Exclusion Act of 1882; 4-5, 8

Family structure, Chinese; 1, 27; linkages 87-89; strains 18-19, 49

Freudenberger, Herbert J. and Richelson, G.; cited 116-117, 119

Funding; 22, 33-34, 69, 105, 132-133; cuts 106-107; grants 96

Gans, Herbert; 13; cited 14

Granovetter, Mark; cited 93-94

Grass-roots organization; 78-80, 82-83, 123, 128, 131-133, 144

Greater Northville Asian Alliance; 77-78

Greater Northville Chinese Association; 145

Greater Northville Legal Services; 144

Hirata, Lucie Cheng; cited 5

Housing; 79, 109, 144; elderly 122-123; problems 12-13; Tenants Group Asociation 37, 144

Housing and Land Association; 37, 144-145

Hui-kuan organization; 87-88

Immigration; 8, 10, 14, 28

Juvenile delinquency, Chinese; 20, 163

Kanter, Rosabeth; cited 43-44

Land encroachment; 13-14, 79; Ace University 13, 32-32, 37-38, 78, 102; Housing and Land Association 37, 144

Language, Chinese; 37, 104, 159

Lewis, Helen, Kobak, Sue and Johnson, Linda; cited 6

Li, Peter; cited 88

Lofland, Lyn H.; cited 1

Lyman, Stanford; cited 1, 22-23, 87

Marxism; 76

Mass media; as farce 17; importance 49

Medicine, Chinese; 21

Meetings, organization; 65-66, 72-74, 115-116

Mu-lan; 126

Mun-yi celebration; 88

Networking; 86-103, 106, 131, 134, 150, 156; compromise 96; extended links 97-99; weak ties 94-95

Northville Chinatown; community linkage 74; factions 108-112; history 8, 10; leadership structure 3-4; living conditions 10-12, 21, 133; map 9

Northville Chinese Women's Club; 29-31, 88, 143

Northville Chinese Life-Enrichment Committee Center; 35, 88, 143; cited 34

Northville North Star; cited v

Payton-Miyasaki, Yuriko; cited 2

Progressive movement; 78, 164-165

Racism; 2-4, 22, 112; Chinese beliefs 30

Role models; 125-128, 132; traditional 126-127

Social events; 31, 39, 76, 143-145

Sung, Betty Lee; cited 2

Support groups; 25-28, 113; community as 43; Chinese 87-89; linkages 86-103, 106, 119, 131-132, 150; women 125

Tenants' Group Association; 37

United States government; impacts 21, 34, 55, 106-107, 133

Values, acculturated; 35-36

Women, Chinese; family importance 45-46, 50, 54, 83-84; lack of social support 17-19, roles of 1, 5-6, 16, 18, 29, 32, 41, 88, 127, 135; sexual discrimination 110-111; stereotypes 5, 121, 129, 132; traditional linkages 86-87, 99, 131

"Women's Culture"; 124-128

Women's Journal (Nu-pao); 127

Wu, Cheng-tu; 75-76

174